Federalist Papers: Jay

John Jay

Bandanna Books • Santa Barbara
2017

Federalist Papers: Jay © Copyright 2017
John Jay Bandanna Books
ISBN 978-0-942208-96-2

WWW.BANDANNABOOKS.COM
CLASSIC LITERATURE • TRANSLATIONS • LANGUAGE

Federalist Papers: Jay

John Jay

Introduction

John Jay was one of the original "Publiu rs, writing five of the first six installments in various New York newspapers that eventually were collected as *The Federalist Papers*, with co-authors Alexander Hamilton and James Madison. All three made essential contributions to the making of the Republic. For health reasons, Jay had not continued his contributions, except for one late entry. An additional essay by Jay is included here, addressed to the same audience, the citizens of New York State.

Jay himself served as the first Chief Justice of the Supreme Court of the new nation, which early became established as an independent arm of government, cognizant of, but standing aloof from, the sometimes creative politicking in this new country trying out a new way of being governed. Politics itself had to be re-invented for the new relationship of citizens to States, and States to Federal government. The *Federalist Papers*, as they came to be called, made an enormous contribution toward shaping a workable democracy not dependent on European or other models of governing, yet extending over a thousand miles of territories with a variety of challenges.

The papers by Hamilton and Madison can be found separately, or all three as a set.

Sasha Newborn
August 2016

Contents

Concerning Dangers from Foreign Force and Influence

For the Independent Journal.

To the People of the State of New York:

When the people of America reflect that they are now called upon to decide a question, which, in its consequences, must prove one of the most important that ever engaged their attention, the propriety of their taking a very comprehensive, as well as a very serious, view of it, will be evident.

Nothing is more certain than the indispensable necessity of government, and it is equally undeniable, that whenever and however it is instituted, the people must cede to it some of their natural rights in order to vest it with requisite powers. It is well worthy of consideration therefore, whether it would conduce more to the interest of the people of America that they should, to all general purposes, be one nation, under one federal government, or that they should divide themselves into separate confederacies, and give to the head of each the same kind of powers which they are advised to place in one national government.

It has until lately been a received and uncontradicted opinion that the prosperity of the people of America depended on their continuing firmly united, and the wishes, prayers, and efforts of our best and wisest citizens have been constantly directed to that object. But politicians now appear, who insist that this opinion is erroneous, and that instead of looking for safety and happiness in union, we ought to seek it in a division of the States into distinct confederacies or sovereignties. However extraordinary this new doctrine may appear, it nevertheless has its advocates; and certain characters who were much opposed to it formerly, are at present of the number. Whatever may be the arguments or inducements which have wrought this change in the sentiments and declarations of these gentlemen, it certainly would not be wise in the people at large to adopt these new political tenets without being fully convinced that they are founded in truth and sound policy.

It has often given me pleasure to observe that independent America was not composed of detached and distant territories, but that one connected, fertile, widespreading country was the portion of our western sons of liberty. Providence has in a particular manner blessed it with a variety of soils and productions, and watered it with innumerable streams, for the delight and accommodation of its inhabitants. A succession of navigable waters forms a kind of chain round its borders, as if to bind it together; while the most noble rivers in the world, running at convenient distances, present them with highways for the easy communication of friendly aids, and the mutual transportation and exchange of their various commodities.

With equal pleasure I have as often taken notice that Providence has been pleased to give this one connected country to one united people--a people descended from the same ancestors, speaking the same language, professing the same religion, attached to the same principles of government, very similar in their manners and customs, and who, by their joint counsels, arms, and efforts, fighting side by side throughout a long and bloody war, have nobly established general liberty and independence.

This country and this people seem to have been made for each other, and it appears as if it was the design of Providence, that an inheritance so proper and convenient for a band of brethren, united to each other by the strongest ties, should never be split into a number of unsocial, jealous, and alien sovereignties.

Similar sentiments have hitherto prevailed among all orders and denominations of men among us. To all general purposes we have uniformly been one people each individual citizen everywhere enjoying the same national rights, privileges, and protection. As a nation we have made peace and war; as a nation we have vanquished our common enemies; as a nation we have formed alliances, and made treaties, and entered into various compacts and conventions with foreign states.

A strong sense of the value and blessings of union induced the people, at a very early period, to institute a federal government to preserve and perpetuate it. They formed it almost as soon as they had a political existence; nay, at a time when their habitations were in flames, when many of their citizens were bleeding, and when the progress of hostility and desolation left little room for those calm and mature inquiries and reflections which must ever precede the formation of a wise and wellbalanced government for a free people. It is not to be wondered at, that a government instituted in times so inauspicious, should on experiment be found greatly deficient and inadequate to the purpose it was intended to answer.

This intelligent people perceived and regretted these defects. Still continuing no less attached to union than enamored of liberty, they observed the danger which immediately threatened the former and more remotely the latter; and being pursuaded that ample security for both could only be found in a national government more wisely framed, they as with one voice, convened the late convention at Philadelphia, to take that important subject under consideration.

This convention composed of men who possessed the confidence of the people, and many of whom had become highly distinguished by their patriotism, virtue and wisdom, in times which tried the minds and hearts of men, undertook the arduous task. In the mild season of peace, with minds unoccupied by other subjects, they passed many months in cool, uninterrupted, and daily consultation; and finally, without having been awed by power, or influenced by any passions except love for their country, they presented and recommended to the people the plan produced by their joint and very unanimous councils.

Admit, for so is the fact, that this plan is only *recommended*, not imposed, yet let it be remembered that it is neither recommended to *blind* approbation, nor to *blind* reprobation; but to that sedate and candid consideration which the magnitude and importance of the subject demand, and which it certainly ought to receive. But this (as was remarked in the foregoing number of this paper) is more to be wished than expected, that it may be so considered and examined. Experience on a former occasion teaches us not to be too sanguine in such hopes. It is not yet forgotten that well-grounded apprehensions of imminent danger induced the people of America to form the memorable Congress of 1774. That body recommended certain measures to their constituents, and the event proved their wisdom; yet it is fresh in our memories how soon the press began to teem with pamphlets and weekly papers against those very measures. Not only many of the officers of government, who obeyed the dictates of personal interest, but others, from a mistaken estimate of consequences, or the undue influence of former attachments, or whose ambition aimed at objects which did not correspond with the public good, were indefatigable in their efforts to pursuade the people to reject the advice of that patriotic Congress. Many, indeed, were deceived and deluded, but the great majority of the people reasoned and decided judiciously; and happy they are in reflecting that they did so.

They considered that the Congress was composed of many wise and experienced men. That, being convened from different parts of the country, they brought with them and communicated to each other a variety of useful information. That, in the course of the time they passed together in inquiring into and discussing the true interests of their country, they must have acquired very accurate knowledge on that head. That they were individually interested in the public liberty and prosperity, and therefore that it was not less their inclination than their duty to recommend only such measures as, after the most mature deliberation, they really thought prudent and advisable.

These and similar considerations then induced the people to rely greatly on the judgment and integrity of the Congress; and they took their advice, notwithstanding the various arts and endeavors used to deter them from it. But if the people at large had reason to confide in the men of that Congress, few of whom had been fully tried or generally known, still greater reason have they now to respect the judgment and advice of the convention, for it is well known that some of the most distinguished members of that Congress, who have been since tried and justly approved for patriotism and abilities, and who have grown old in acquiring political information, were also members of this convention, and carried into it their accumulated knowledge and experience.

It is worthy of remark that not only the first, but every succeeding Congress, as well as the late convention, have invariably joined with the people in thinking that the prosperity of America depended on its Union. To preserve and perpetuate it was the great object of the people in forming that convention, and it is also the great object of the plan which the convention has advised them to adopt. With what propriety, therefore, or for what good purposes, are attempts at this particular period made by some men to depreciate the importance of the Union? Or why is it suggested that three or four confederacies would be better than one? I am persuaded in my own mind that the people have always thought right on this subject, and that their universal and uniform attachment to the cause of the Union rests on great and weighty reasons, which I shall endeavor to develop and explain in some ensuing papers. They who promote the idea of substituting a number of distinct confederacies in the room of the plan of the convention, seem clearly to foresee that the rejection of it would put the continuance of the Union in the utmost jeopardy. That certainly would be the case, and I sincerely wish that it may be as clearly foreseen by every good citizen, that whenever the dissolution of the Union arrives, America will have reason to exclaim, in the words of the poet:

"Farewell!
A Long Farewell to All My Greatness."

PUBLIUS

FEDERALIST No. 3

The Same Subject Continued

(Concerning Dangers From Foreign Force and Influence)

For the Independent Journal.

To the People of the State of New York:

It is not a new observation that the people of any country (if, like the Americans, intelligent and wellinformed) seldom adopt and steadily persevere for many years in an erroneous opinion respecting their interests. That consideration naturally tends to create great respect for the high opinion which the people of America have so long and uniformly entertained of the importance of their continuing firmly united under one federal government, vested with sufficient powers for all general and national purposes.

The more attentively I consider and investigate the reasons which appear to have given birth to this opinion, the more I become convinced that they are cogent and conclusive. Among the many objects to which a wise and free people find it necessary to direct their attention, that of providing for their *safety* seems to be the first. The *safety* of the people doubtless has relation to a great variety of circumstances and considerations, and consequently affords great latitude to those who wish to define it precisely and comprehensively.

At present I mean only to consider it as it respects

security for the preservation of peace and tranquillity, as well as against dangers from *foreign arms and influence*, as from dangers of the *like kind* arising from domestic causes. As the former of these comes first in order, it is proper it should be the first discussed. Let us therefore proceed to examine whether the people are not right in their opinion that a cordial Union, under an efficient national government, affords them the best security that can be devised against *hostilities* from abroad.

The number of wars which have happened or will happen in the world will always be found to be in proportion to the number and weight of the causes, whether *real* or *pretended*, which *provoke* or *invite* them. If this remark be just, it becomes useful to inquire whether so many *just* causes of war are likely to be given by *United America* as by *Disunited* America; for if it should turn out that United America will probably give the fewest, then it will follow that in this respect the Union tends most to preserve the people in a state of peace with other nations.

The *just* causes of war, for the most part, arise either from violation of treaties or from direct violence. America has already formed treaties with no less than six foreign nations, and all of them, except Prussia, are maritime, and therefore able to annoy and injure us. She has also extensive commerce with Portugal, Spain, and Britain, and, with respect to the two latter, has, in addition, the circumstance of neighborhood to attend to. It is of high importance to the peace of America that she observe the laws of nations towards all these powers, and to me it appears evident that this will be more perfectly and punctually done by one national government than it could be either by thirteen separate States or by three or four distinct confederacies.

Because when once an efficient national government is established, the best men in the country will not only consent to serve, but also will generally be appointed to manage it; for, although town or country, or other contracted influence, may place men in State assemblies, or senates, or courts of justice, or executive departments, yet more general and extensive reputation for talents and other qualifications will be necessary to recommend men to offices under the national government,--especially as it will have the widest field for choice, and never experience that want of proper persons which is not uncommon in some of the States. Hence, it will result that the administration, the political counsels, and the judicial decisions of the national government will be more wise, systematical, and judicious than those of individual States, and consequently more satisfactory with respect to other nations, as well as more *safe* with respect to us.

Because, under the national government, treaties and articles of treaties, as well as the laws of nations, will always be expounded in one sense and executed in the same manner,--whereas, adjudications on the same points and questions, in thirteen States, or in three or four confederacies, will not always accord or be consistent; and that, as well from the variety of independent courts and judges appointed by different and independent governments, as from the different local laws and interests which may affect and influence them. The wisdom of the convention, in committing such questions to the jurisdiction and judgment of courts appointed by and responsible only to one national government, cannot be too much commended.

Because the prospect of present loss or advantage may often tempt the governing party in one or two States to swerve from good faith and justice; but those temptations, not reaching the other States, and consequently having little or no influence on the national government, the temptation will be fruitless, and good faith and justice be preserved. The case of the treaty of peace with Britain adds great weight to this reasoning.

Because, even if the governing party in a State should be disposed to resist such temptations, yet as such temptations may, and commonly do, result from circumstances peculiar to the State, and may affect a great number of the inhabitants, the governing party may not always be able, if willing, to prevent the injustice meditated, or to punish the aggressors. But the national government, not being affected by those local circumstances, will neither be induced to commit the wrong themselves, nor want power or inclination to prevent or punish its commission by others.

So far, therefore, as either designed or accidental violations of treaties and the laws of nations afford *just* causes of war, they are less to be apprehended under one general government than under several lesser ones, and in that respect the former most favors the *safety* of the people.

As to those just causes of war which proceed from direct and unlawful violence, it appears equally clear to me that one good national government affords vastly more security against dangers of that sort than can be derived from any other quarter.

Because such violences are more frequently caused by the passions and interests of a part than of the whole; of one or two States than of the Union. Not a single Indian war has yet been occasioned by aggressions of the present federal government, feeble as it is; but there are several instances of Indian hostilities having been provoked by the improper conduct of individual States, who, either unable or unwilling to restrain or punish offenses, have given occasion to the slaughter of many innocent inhabitants.

The neighborhood of Spanish and British territories, bordering on some States and not on others, naturally confines the causes of quarrel more immediately to the borderers. The bordering States, if any, will be those who, under the impulse of sudden irritation, and a quick sense of apparent interest or injury, will be most likely, by direct violence, to excite war with these nations; and nothing can so effectually obviate that danger as a national government, whose wisdom and prudence will not be diminished by the passions which actuate the parties immediately interested.

But not only fewer just causes of war will be given by the national government, but it will also be more in their power to accommodate and settle them amicably. They will be more temperate and cool, and in that respect, as well as in others, will be more in capacity to act advisedly than the offending State. The pride of states, as well as of men, naturally disposes them to justify all their actions, and opposes their acknowledging, correcting, or repairing their errors and offenses. The national government, in such cases, will not be affected by this pride, but will proceed with moderation and candor to consider and decide on the means most proper to extricate them from the difficulties which threaten them.

Besides, it is well known that acknowledgments, explanations, and compensations are often accepted as satisfactory from a strong united nation, which would be rejected as unsatisfactory if offered by a State or confederacy of little consideration or power.

In the year 1685, the state of Genoa having offended Louis XIV, endeavored to appease him. He demanded that they should send their Doge, or chief magistrate, accompanied by four of their senators, to *France*, to ask his pardon and receive his terms. They were obliged to submit to it for the sake of peace. Would he on any occasion either have demanded or have received the like humiliation from Spain, or Britain, or any other *powerful* nation?

PUBLIUS

The Same Subject Continued

(Concerning Dangers From Foreign Force and Influence)

For the Independent Journal.

To the People of the State of New York:

My last paper assigned several reasons why the safety of the people would be best secured by union against the danger it may be exposed to by *just* causes of war given to other nations; and those reasons show that such causes would not only be more rarely given, but would also be more easily accommodated, by a national government than either by the State governments or the proposed little confederacies.

But the safety of the people of America against dangers from *foreign* force depends not only on their forbearing to give *just* causes of war to other nations, but also on their placing and continuing themselves in such a situation as not to *invite* hostility or insult; for it need not be observed that there are *pretended* as well as just causes of war.

It is too true, however disgraceful it may be to human nature, that nations in general will make war whenever they have a prospect of getting anything by it; nay, absolute monarchs will often make war when their nations are to get nothing by it, but for the purposes and objects merely personal, such as thirst for military glory, revenge for personal affronts, ambition, or private compacts to aggrandize or support their particular families or partisans. These and a variety of other motives, which affect only the mind of the sovereign, often lead him to engage in wars not sanctified by justice or the voice and interests of his people. But, independent of these inducements to war, which are more prevalent in absolute monarchies, but which well deserve our attention, there are others which affect nations as often as kings; and some of them will on examination be found to grow out of our relative situation and circumstances.

With France and with Britain we are rivals in the fisheries, and can supply their markets cheaper than they can themselves, notwithstanding any efforts to prevent it by bounties on their own or duties on foreign fish.

With them and with most other European nations we are rivals in navigation and the carrying trade; and we shall deceive ourselves if we suppose that any of them will rejoice to see it flourish; for, as our carrying trade cannot increase without in some degree diminishing theirs, it is more their interest, and will be more their policy, to restrain than to promote it.

In the trade to China and India, we interfere with more than one nation, inasmuch as it enables us to partake in advantages which they had in a manner monopolized, and as we thereby supply ourselves with commodities which we used to purchase from them.

The extension of our own commerce in our own vessels cannot give pleasure to any nations who possess territories on or near this continent, because the cheapness and excellence of our productions, added to the circumstance of vicinity, and the enterprise and address of our merchants and navigators, will give us a greater share in the advantages which those territories afford, than consists with the wishes or policy of their respective sovereigns.

Spain thinks it convenient to shut the Mississippi against us on the one side, and Britain excludes us from the Saint Lawrence on the other; nor will either of them permit the other waters which are between them and us to become the means of mutual intercourse and traffic.

From these and such like considerations, which might, if consistent with prudence, be more amplified and detailed, it is easy to see that jealousies and uneasinesses may gradually slide into the minds and cabinets of other nations, and that we are not to expect that they should regard our advancement in union, in power and consequence by land and by sea, with an eye of indifference and composure.

The people of America are aware that inducements to war may arise out of these circumstances, as well as from others not so obvious at present, and that whenever such inducements may find fit time and opportunity for operation, pretenses to color and justify them will not be wanting. Wisely, therefore, do they consider union and a good national government as necessary to put and keep them in *such a situation* as, instead of *inviting* war, will tend to repress and discourage it. That situation consists in the best possible state of defense, and necessarily depends on the government, the arms, and the resources of the country.

As the safety of the whole is the interest of the whole, and cannot be provided for without government, either one or more or many, let us inquire whether one good government is not, relative to the object in question, more competent than any other given number whatever.

One government can collect and avail itself of the talents and experience of the ablest men, in whatever part of the Union they may be found. It can move on uniform principles of policy. It can harmonize, assimilate, and protect the several parts and members, and extend the benefit of its foresight and precautions to each. In the formation of treaties, it will regard the interest of the whole, and the particular interests of the parts as connected with that of the whole. It can apply the resources and power of the whole to the defense of any particular part, and that more easily and expeditiously than State governments or separate confederacies can possibly do, for want of concert and unity of system. It can place the militia under one plan of discipline, and, by putting their officers in a proper line of subordination to the Chief Magistrate, will, as it were, consolidate them into one corps, and thereby render them more efficient than if divided into thirteen or into three or four distinct independent companies.

What would the militia of Britain be if the English militia obeyed the government of England, if the Scotch militia obeyed the government of Scotland, and if the Welsh militia obeyed the government of Wales? Suppose an invasion; would those three governments (if they agreed at all) be able, with all their respective forces, to operate against the enemy so effectually as the single government of Great Britain would?

We have heard much of the fleets of Britain, and the time may come, if we are wise, when the fleets of America may engage attention. But if one national government, had not so regulated the navigation of Britain as to make it a nursery for seamen--if one national government had not called forth all the national means and materials for forming fleets, their prowess and their thunder would never have been celebrated. Let England have its navigation and fleet--let Scotland have its navigation and fleet--let Wales have its navigation and fleet--let Ireland have its navigation and fleet--let those four of the constituent parts of the British empire be under four independent governments, and it is easy to perceive how soon they would each dwindle into comparative insignificance.

Apply these facts to our own case. Leave America divided into thirteen or, if you please, into three or four independent governments--what armies could they raise and pay--what fleets could they ever hope to have? If one was attacked, would the others fly to its succor, and spend their blood and money in its defense? Would there be no danger of their being flattered into neutrality by its specious promises, or seduced by a too great fondness for peace to decline hazarding their tranquillity and present safety for the sake of neighbors, of whom perhaps they have been jealous, and whose importance they are content to see diminished? Although such conduct would not be wise, it would, nevertheless, be natural. The history of the states of Greece, and of other countries, abounds with such instances, and it is not improbable that what has so often happened would, under similar circumstances, happen again.

But admit that they might be willing to help the invaded State or confederacy. How, and when, and in what proportion shall aids of men and money be afforded? Who shall command the allied armies, and from which of them shall he receive his orders? Who shall settle the terms of peace, and in case of disputes what umpire shall decide between them and compel acquiescence? Various difficulties and inconveniences would be inseparable from such a situation; whereas one government, watching over the general and common interests, and combining and directing the powers and resources of the whole, would be free from all these embarrassments, and conduce far more to the safety of the people.

But whatever may be our situation, whether firmly united under one national government, or split into a number of confederacies, certain it is, that foreign nations will know and view it exactly as it is; and they will act toward us accordingly. If they see that our national government is efficient and well administered, our trade prudently regulated, our militia properly organized and disciplined, our resources and finances discreetly managed, our credit re-established, our people free, contented, and united, they will be much more disposed to cultivate our friendship than provoke our resentment. If, on the other hand, they find us either destitute of an effectual government (each State doing right or wrong, as to its rulers may seem convenient), or split into three or four independent and probably discordant republics or confederacies, one inclining to Britain, another to France, and a third to Spain, and perhaps played off against each other by the three, what a poor, pitiful figure will America make in their eyes! How liable would she become not only to their contempt but to their outrage, and how soon would dear-bought experience proclaim that when a people or family so divide, it never fails to be against themselves.

PUBLIUS

The Same Subject Continued

(Concerning Dangers From Foreign Force and Influence)

For the Independent Journal.

To the People of the State of New York:

Queen Anne, in her letter of the 1st July, 1706, to the Scotch Parliament, makes some observations on the importance of the *Union* then forming between England and Scotland, which merit our attention. I shall present the public with one or two extracts from it: "An entire and perfect union will be the solid foundation of lasting peace: It will secure your religion, liberty, and property; remove the animosities amongst yourselves, and the jealousies and differences betwixt our two kingdoms. It must increase your strength, riches, and trade; and by this union the whole island, being joined in affection and free from all apprehensions of different interest, will be *enabled to resist all its enemies.*" "We most earnestly recommend to you calmness and unanimity in this great and weighty affair, that the union may be brought to a happy conclusion, being the only *effectual* way to secure our present and future happiness, and disappoint the designs of our and your enemies, who will doubtless, on this occasion, *Use their utmost endeavors to prevent or delay this Union.*"

It was remarked in the preceding paper, that weakness and divisions at home would invite dangers from abroad; and that nothing would tend more to secure us from them than union, strength, and good government within ourselves. This subject is copious and cannot easily be exhausted.

The history of Great Britain is the one with which we are in general the best acquainted, and it gives us many useful lessons. We may profit by their experience without paying the price which it cost them. Although it seems obvious to common sense that the people of such an island should be but one nation, yet we find that they were for ages divided into three, and that those three were almost constantly embroiled in quarrels and wars with one another. Notwithstanding their true interest with respect to the continental nations was really the same, yet by the arts and policy and practices of those nations, their mutual jealousies were perpetually kept inflamed, and for a long series of years they were far more inconvenient and troublesome than they were useful and assisting to each other.

Should the people of America divide themselves into three or four nations, would not the same thing happen? Would not similar jealousies arise, and be in like manner cherished? Instead of their being "joined in affection" and free from all apprehension of different "interests," envy and jealousy would soon extinguish confidence and affection, and the partial interests of each confederacy, instead of the general interests of all America, would be the only objects of their policy and pursuits. Hence, like most other *bordering* nations, they would always be either involved in disputes and war, or live in the constant apprehension of them.

The most sanguine advocates for three or four confederacies cannot reasonably suppose that they would long remain exactly on an equal footing in point of strength, even if it was possible to form them so at first; but, admitting that to be practicable, yet what human contrivance can secure the continuance of such equality? Independent of those local circumstances which tend to beget and increase power in one part and to impede its progress in another, we must advert to the effects of that superior policy and good management which would probably distinguish the government of one above the rest, and by which their relative equality in strength and consideration would be destroyed. For it cannot be presumed that the same degree of sound policy, prudence, and foresight would uniformly be observed by each of these confederacies for a long succession of years.

Whenever, and from whatever causes, it might happen, and happen it would, that any one of these nations or confederacies should rise on the scale of political importance much above the degree of her neighbors, that moment would those neighbors behold her with envy and with fear. Both those passions would lead them to countenance, if not to promote, whatever might promise to diminish her importance; and would also restrain them from measures calculated to advance or even to secure her prosperity. Much time would not be necessary to enable her to discern these unfriendly dispositions. She would soon begin, not only to lose confidence in her neighbors, but also to feel a disposition equally unfavorable to them. Distrust naturally creates distrust, and by nothing is good-will and kind conduct more speedily changed than by invidious jealousies and uncandid imputations, whether expressed or implied.

The North is generally the region of strength, and many local circumstances render it probable that the most Northern of the proposed confederacies would, at a period not very distant, be unquestionably more formidable than any of the others. No sooner would this become evident than the *Northern hive* would excite the same ideas and sensations in the more southern parts of America which it formerly did in the southern parts of Europe. Nor does it appear to be a rash conjecture that its young swarms might often be tempted to gather honey in the more blooming fields and milder air of their luxurious and more delicate neighbors.

They who well consider the history of similar divisions and confederacies will find abundant reason to apprehend that those in contemplation would in no other sense be neighbors than as they would be borderers; that they would neither love nor trust one another, but on the contrary would be a prey to discord, jealousy, and mutual injuries; in short, that they would place us exactly in the situations in which some nations doubtless wish to see us, viz., *formidable only to each other*.

From these considerations it appears that those gentlemen are greatly mistaken who suppose that alliances offensive and defensive might be formed between these confederacies, and would produce that combination and union of wills of arms and of resources, which would be necessary to put and keep them in a formidable state of defense against foreign enemies. When did the independent states, into which Britain and Spain were formerly divided, combine in such alliance, or unite their forces against a foreign enemy? The proposed confederacies will be *distinct nations*. Each of them would have its commerce with foreigners to regulate by distinct treaties; and as their productions and commodities are different and proper for different markets, so would those treaties be essentially different. Different commercial concerns must create different interests, and of course different degrees of political attachment to and connection with different foreign nations. Hence it might and probably would happen that the foreign nation with whom the *Southern* confederacy might be at war would be the one with whom the *Northern* confederacy would be the most desirous of preserving peace and friendship. An alliance so contrary to their immediate interest would not therefore be easy to form, nor, if formed, would it be observed and fulfilled with perfect good faith.

Nay, it is far more probable that in America, as in Europe, neighboring nations, acting under the impulse of opposite interests and unfriendly passions, would frequently be found taking different sides. Considering our distance from Europe, it would be more natural for these confederacies to apprehend danger from one another than from distant nations, and therefore that each of them should be more desirous to guard against the others by the aid of foreign alliances, than to guard against foreign dangers by alliances between themselves. And here let us not forget how much more easy it is to receive foreign fleets into our ports, and foreign armies into our country, than it is to persuade or compel them to depart. How many conquests did the Romans and others make in the characters of allies, and what innovations did they under the same character introduce into the governments of those whom they pretended to protect.

Let candid men judge, then, whether the division of America into any given number of independent sovereignties would tend to secure us against the hostilities and improper interference of foreign nations.

PUBLIUS

The Powers of the Senate

From the New York Packet.
Friday, March 7, 1788.

To the People of the State of New York:

It is a just and not a new observation, that enemies to particular persons, and opponents to particular measures, seldom confine their censures to such things only in either as are worthy of blame. Unless on this principle, it is difficult to explain the motives of their conduct, who condemn the proposed Constitution in the aggregate, and treat with severity some of the most unexceptionable articles in it. The second section gives power to the President, "*by and with the advice and consent of the Senate, to make treaties, provided two-thirds of the Senators present concur.*"

The power of making treaties is an important one, especially as it relates to war, peace, and commerce; and it should not be delegated but in such a mode, and with such precautions, as will afford the highest security that it will be exercised by men the best qualified for the purpose, and in the manner most conducive to the public good. The convention appears to have been attentive to both these points: they have directed the President to be chosen by select bodies of electors, to be deputed by the people for that express purpose; and they have committed the appointment of senators to the State legislatures. This mode has, in such cases, vastly the advantage of elections by the people in their collective capacity, where the activity of party zeal, taking the advantage of the supineness, the ignorance, and the hopes and fears of the unwary and interested, often places men in office by the votes of a small proportion of the electors.

As the select assemblies for choosing the President, as well as the State legislatures who appoint the senators, will in general be composed of the most enlightened and respectable citizens, there is reason to presume that their attention and their votes will be directed to those men only who have become the most distinguished by their abilities and virtue, and in whom the people perceive just grounds for confidence. The Constitution manifests very particular attention to this object. By excluding men under thirty-five from the first office, and those under thirty from the second, it confines the electors to men of whom the people have had time to form a judgment, and with respect to whom they will not be liable to be deceived by those brilliant appearances of genius and patriotism, which, like transient meteors, sometimes mislead as well as dazzle. If the observation be well founded, that wise kings will always be served by able ministers, it is fair to argue, that as an assembly of select electors possess, in a greater degree than kings, the means of extensive and accurate information relative to men and characters, so will their appointments bear at least equal marks of discretion and discernment. The inference which naturally results from these considerations is this, that the President and senators so chosen will always be of the number of those who best understand our national interests, whether considered in relation to the several States or to foreign nations, who are best able to promote those interests, and whose reputation for integrity inspires and merits confidence. With such men the power of making treaties may be safely lodged.

Although the absolute necessity of system, in the conduct of any business, is universally known and acknowledged, yet the high importance of it in national affairs has not yet become sufficiently impressed on the public mind.

They who wish to commit the power under consideration to a popular assembly, composed of members constantly coming and going in quick succession, seem not to recollect that such a body must necessarily be inadequate to the attainment of those great objects, which require to be steadily contemplated in all their relations and circumstances, and which can only be approached and achieved by measures which not only talents, but also exact information, and often much time, are necessary to concert and to execute. It was wise, therefore, in the convention to provide, not only that the power of making treaties should be committed to able and honest men, but also that they should continue in place a sufficient time to become perfectly acquainted with our national concerns, and to form and introduce a a system for the management of them. The duration prescribed is such as will give them an opportunity of greatly extending their political information, and of rendering their accumulating experience more and more beneficial to their country. Nor has the convention discovered less prudence in providing for the frequent elections of senators in such a way as to obviate the inconvenience of periodically transferring those great affairs entirely to new men; for by leaving a considerable residue of the old ones in place, uniformity and order, as well as a constant succession of official information will be preserved.

There are a few who will not admit that the affairs of trade and navigation should be regulated by a system cautiously formed and steadily pursued; and that both our treaties and our laws should correspond with and be made to promote it. It is of much consequence that this correspondence and conformity be carefully maintained; and they who assent to the truth of this position will see and confess that it is well provided for by making concurrence of the Senate necessary both to treaties and to laws.

It seldom happens in the negotiation of treaties, of whatever nature, but that perfect *secrecy* and immediate *despatch* are sometimes requisite. These are cases where the most useful intelligence may be obtained, if the persons possessing it can be relieved from apprehensions of discovery. Those apprehensions will operate on those persons whether they are actuated by mercenary or friendly motives; and there doubtless are many of both descriptions, who would rely on the secrecy of the President, but who would not confide in that of the Senate, and still less in that of a large popular Assembly. The convention have done well, therefore, in so disposing of the power of making treaties, that although the President must, in forming them, act by the advice and consent of the Senate, yet he will be able to manage the business of intelligence in such a manner as prudence may suggest. They who have turned their attention to the affairs of men, must have perceived that there are tides in them; tides very irregular in their duration, strength, and direction, and seldom found to run twice exactly in the same manner or measure. To discern and to profit by these tides in national affairs is the business of those who preside over them; and they who have had much experience on this head inform us, that there frequently are occasions when days, nay, even when hours, are precious. The loss of a battle, the death of a prince, the removal of a minister, or other circumstances intervening to change the present posture and aspect of affairs, may turn the most favorable tide into a course opposite to our wishes. As in the field, so in the cabinet, there are moments to be seized as they pass, and they who preside in either should be left in capacity to improve them. So often and so essentially have we heretofore suffered from the want of secrecy and despatch, that the Constitution would have been inexcusably defective, if no attention had been paid to those objects. Those matters which in negotiations usually require the most secrecy and the most despatch, are those preparatory and auxiliary measures which are not otherwise important in a national view, than as they tend to facilitate the attainment of the objects of the negotiation. For these, the President will find no difficulty to provide; and should any circumstance occur which requires the advice and consent of the Senate, he may at any time convene them. Thus we see that the Constitution provides that our negotiations for treaties shall have every advantage which can be derived from talents, information, integrity, and deliberate investigations, on the one hand, and from secrecy and despatch on the other.

But to this plan, as to most others that have ever appeared, objections are contrived and urged. Some are displeased with it, not on account of any errors or defects in it, but because, as the treaties, when made, are to have the force of laws, they should be made only by men invested with legislative authority. These gentlemen seem not to consider that the judgments of our courts, and the commissions constitutionally given by our governor, are as valid and as binding on all persons whom they concern, as the laws passed by our legislature. All constitutional acts of power, whether in the executive or in the judicial department, have as much legal validity and obligation as if they proceeded from the legislature; and therefore, whatever name be given to the power of making treaties, or however obligatory they may be when made, certain it is, that the people may, with much propriety, commit the power to a distinct body from the legislature, the executive, or the judicial. It surely does not follow, that because they have given the power of making laws to the legislature, that therefore they should likewise give them the power to do every other act of sovereignty by which the citizens are to be bound and affected.

Others, though content that treaties should be made in the mode proposed, are averse to their being the *supreme* laws of the land. They insist, and profess to believe, that treaties like acts of assembly, should be repealable at pleasure. This idea seems to be new and peculiar to this country, but new errors, as well as new truths, often appear. These gentlemen would do well to reflect that a treaty is only another name for a bargain, and that it would be impossible to find a nation who would make any bargain with us, which should be binding on them *absolutely*, but on us only so long and so far as we may think proper to be bound by it. They who make laws may, without doubt, amend or repeal them; and it will not be disputed that they who make treaties may alter or cancel them; but still let us not forget that treaties are made, not by only one of the contracting parties, but by both; and consequently, that as the consent of both was essential to their formation at first, so must it ever afterwards be to alter or cancel them. The proposed Constitution, therefore, has not in the least extended the obligation of treaties. They are just as binding, and just as far beyond the lawful reach of legislative acts now, as they will be at any future period, or under any form of government.

However useful jealousy may be in republics, yet when like bile in the natural, it abounds too much in the body politic, the eyes of both become very liable to be deceived by the delusive appearances which that malady casts on surrounding objects. From this cause, probably, proceed the fears and apprehensions of some, that the President and Senate may make treaties without an equal eye to the interests of all the States. Others suspect that two thirds will oppress the remaining third, and ask whether those gentlemen are made sufficiently responsible for their conduct; whether, if they act corruptly, they can be punished; and if they make disadvantageous treaties, how are we to get rid of those treaties? As all the States are equally represented in the Senate, and by men the most able and the most willing to promote the interests of their constituents, they will all have an equal degree of influence in that body, especially while they continue to be careful in appointing proper persons, and to insist on their punctual attendance. In proportion as the United States assume a national form and a national character, so will the good of the whole be more and more an object of attention, and the government must be a weak one indeed, if it should forget that the good of the whole can only be promoted by advancing the good of each of the parts or members which compose the whole. It will not be in the power of the President and Senate to make any treaties by which they and their families and estates will not be equally bound and affected with the rest of the community; and, having no private interests distinct from that of the nation, they will be under no temptations to neglect the latter.

As to corruption, the case is not supposable. He must either have been very unfortunate in his intercourse with the world, or possess a heart very susceptible of such impressions, who can think it probable that the President and two thirds of the Senate will ever be capable of such unworthy conduct. The idea is too gross and too invidious to be entertained. But in such a case, if it should ever happen, the treaty so obtained from us would, like all other fraudulent contracts, be null and void by the law of nations. With respect to their responsibility, it is difficult to conceive how it could be increased. Every consideration that can influence the human mind, such as honor, oaths, reputations, conscience, the love of country, and family affections and attachments, afford security for their fidelity. In short, as the Constitution has taken the utmost care that they shall be men of talents and integrity, we have reason to be persuaded that the treaties they make will be as advantageous as, all circumstances considered, could be made; and so far as the fear of punishment and disgrace can operate, that motive to good behavior is amply afforded by the article on the subject of impeachments.

PUBLIUS

John Jay made additional comments during and after the contention over the Bill of Rights, signed with his own name, rather than as "Publius," the pseudonym shared by Alexander Hamilton and James Madison. A few of these on the same subjects are included here, as well as some back-and-forth discussions when he sits as as the first Chief Justice of the Supreme Court.

AN ADDRESS TO THE PEOPLE
OF THE STATE OF NEW YORK

an additional essay by John Jay

Friends and Fellow-Citizens:

There are times and seasons when general evils spread general alarm and uneasiness, and yet arise from causes too complicated and too little understood by many to produce a unanimity of opinions respecting their remedies. Hence it is that on such occasions the conflict of arguments too often excites a conflict of passions, and introduces a degree of discord and animosity which, by agitating the public mind, dispose it to precipitation and extravagance. They who on the ocean have been unexpectedly enveloped with tempests, or suddenly entangled among rocks and shoals, know the value of that serene self-possession and presence of mind to which in such cases they owed their preservation; nor will the heroes who have given us victory and peace hesitate to acknowledge that we are as much indebted for those blessings to the calm prevision and cool intrepidity which planned and conducted our military measures, as to the glowing animation with which they were executed.

While reason retains her rule, while men are as ready to receive as to give advice, and as willing to be convinced themselves as to convince others, there are few political evils from which a free and enlightened people cannot deliver themselves. It is unquestionably true that the great body of the people love their country, and with it prosperity; and this observation is particularly applicable to the people of a free country, for they have more and stronger reasons for loving it than others. It is not, therefore, to vicious motives that the unhappy divisions which sometime prevail among them are to be imputed; the people at large always mean well, and although they may on certain occasions be misled by the counsels or injured by the efforts of the few who expect more advantage from the wreck than from the preservation of national prosperity, yet the motives of these few are by no means to be confounded with those of the community in general.

That such seeds of discord and danger have been disseminated and begin to take root in America as, unless eradicated, will soon poison our gardens and our fields, is a truth much to be lamented; and the more so as their growth rapidly increases while we are wasting the season in honestly but imprudently disputing, not whether they shall be pulled up, but by whom, in what manner, and with what instruments the work shall be done.

When the King of Great Britain, misguided by men who did not merit his confidence, asserted the unjust claim of binding us in all cases whatsoever, and prepared to obtain our submission by force, the object which engrossed our attention, however important, was nevertheless plain and simple. "What shall be done?" was the question; the people answered, "Let us unite our counsels and our arms." They sent delegates to Congress and soldiers to the field. Confiding in the probity and wisdom of Congress, they received their recommendations as if they had been laws; and that ready acquiescence in their advice enabled those patriots to save their country. Then there was little leisure or disposition for controversy respecting the expediency of measures; hostile fleets soon filled our ports, and hostile armies spread desolation on our shores. Union was then considered as the most essential of human means, and we almost worshipped it with as much fervor as pagans in distress implored the protection of their tutelar deities. That Union was the child of wisdom. Heaven blessed it and wrought out our political salvation.

That glorious war was succeeded by an advantageous peace. When danger disappeared, ease, tranquillity, and a sense of security loosened the bonds of union; and Congress and soldiers and good faith depreciated with their apparent importance. Recommendations lost their influence, and requisitions were rendered nugatory, not by their want of propriety, but by their want of power. The spirit of private gain expelled the spirit of public good, and men became more intent on the means of enriching and aggrandizing themselves than of enriching and aggrandizing their country. Hence the war-worn veteran, whose reward for toil and wounds existed in written promises, found Congress without the means, and too many States without the disposition, to do him justice. Hard necessity compelled him, and others under similar circumstances, to sell their honest claims on the public for a little bread; and thus unmerited misfortunes and patriotic distresses became articles of speculation and commerce.

These and many other evils, too well known to require enumeration, imperceptibly stole in upon us, and acquired an unhappy influence on our public affairs. But such evils, like the worst of weeds, will naturally spring up in so rich a soil; and a good government is as necessary to subdue the one, as an attentive gardener or husbandman is to destroy the other. Even the garden of Paradise required to be dressed, and while men continue to be constantly impelled to error and to wrong by innumerable circumstances and temptations, so long will society experience the increasing necessity of government.

It is a pity that the expectations which actuated the authors of the existing Confederation neither have nor can be realized. Accustomed to see and admire the glorious spirit which moved all ranks of people in the most gloomy moments of the war, observing their steadfast attachment to union, and the wisdom they so often manifested both in choosing and confiding in their rulers, these gentlemen were led to flatter themselves that the people of America only required to know what ought to be done, to do it. This amiable mistake induced them to institute a national government in such a manner as, though very fit to give advice, was yet destitute of power, and so constructed as to be very unfit to be trusted with it. They seem not to have been sensible that mere advice is a bad substitute for laws; nor to have recollected that the advice even of the all-wise and best of Beings has been always disregarded by a great majority of all the men that ever lived.

Experience is a severe preceptor, but it teaches useful truths, and, however harsh, is always honest. Be calm and dispassionate and listen to what it tells us.

Prior to the revolution we had little occasion to inquire or know much about national affairs, for although they existed and were managed, yet they were managed for us and not by us. Intent on our domestic concerns, our internal legislative business, our agriculture, and our buying and selling, we were seldom anxious about what passed or was doing in foreign courts. As we had nothing to do with the department of policy, so the affairs of it were not-detailed to us, and we took as little pains to inform ourselves as others did to inform us of them. War and peace, alliances and treaties, and commerce and navigation were conducted and regulated without our advice or control. While we had liberty and justice, and in security enjoyed the fruits of our "vine and fig-tree," we were in general too content and too much occupied to be at the trouble of investigating the various political combinations in this department, or to examine and perceive how exceedingly important they often were to the advancement and protection of our prosperity. This habit and turn of thinking affords one reason why so much more care was taken, and so much more wisdom displayed, in forming our State governments than in forming our Federal or national one.

By the Confederation as it now stands, the direction of

general and national affairs is committed to a single body of men—*viz.*, the Congress. They may make war, but they are not empowered to raise men or money to carry it on. They may make peace, but without the means to see the terms of it observed. They may form alliances, but without ability to comply with the stipulations on their part. They may enter into treaties of commerce, but without power to enforce them at home or abroad. They may borrow money, but without having the means of repayment. They may partly regulate commerce, but without authority to execute their ordinances. They may appoint ministers and other officers of trust, but without power to try or punish them for misdemeanors. They may resolve, but cannot execute either with despatch or with secrecy. In short, they may consult, and deliberate, and recommend, and make requisitions, and they who please may regard them.

From this new and wonderful system of government it has come to pass that almost every national object of every kind is at this day unprovided for; and other nations, taking the advantage of its imbecility, are daily multiplying commercial restraints upon us. Our fur trade is gone to Canada, and British garrisons keep the keys of it. Our ship-yards have almost ceased to disturb the repose of the neighborhood by the noise of the axe and the hammer; and while foreign flags fly triumphantly above our highest houses, the American stars seldom do more than shed a few feeble rays about the humbler masts of river sloops and coasting schooners. The greater part of our hardy seamen are ploughing the ocean in foreign pay, and not a few of our ingenious shipwrights are now building vessels on alien shores. Although our increasing agriculture and industry extend and multiply our productions, yet they constantly diminish in value; and although we permit all nations to fill our country with their merchandises, yet their best markets are shut against us. Is there an English, or a French, or a Spanish island or port in the West Indies to which an American vessel can carry a cargo of flour for sale? Not one. The Algerines exclude us from the Mediterranean and adjacent countries; and we are neither able to purchase nor to command the free use of those seas. Can our little towns or larger cities consume the immense productions of our fertile country? or will they without trade be able to pay a good price for the proportion which they do consume? The last season gave a very unequivocal answer to those questions. What numbers of fine cattle have returned from this city to the country for want of buyers? What great quantities of salted and other provisions still lie useless in the stores? To how much below the former price is our corn, and wheat, and flour, and lumber rapidly falling? Our debts remain undiminished, and the interest on them accumulating; our credit abroad is nearly extinguished, and at home unrestored; they who had money have sent it beyond the reach of our laws, and scarcely any man can borrow of his neighbor. Nay, does not experience also tell us that it is as difficult to pay as to borrow; that even our houses and lands cannot command money; that law-suits and usurious contracts abound; that our farms fall on executions for less than half their value; and that distress in various forms and in various ways is approaching fast to the doors of our best citizens?

These things have been gradually coming upon us ever since the peace; they have been perceived and proclaimed, but the universal rage and pursuit of private gain conspired, with other causes, to prevent any proper efforts being made to meliorate our condition by due attention to our national affairs, until the late Convention was convened for that purpose. From the result of their deliberations, the States expected to derive much good, and should they be disappointed, it will probably be not less their misfortune than their fault. That Convention was in general composed of excellent and tried men—men who had become conspicuous for their wisdom and public services, and whose names and characters will be venerated by posterity. Generous and candid minds cannot perceive without pain the illiberal manner in which some have taken the liberty to treat them, nor forbear to impute it to impure and improper motives. Zeal for public good, like zeal for religion, may sometimes carry men beyond the bounds of reason, but it is not conceivable that on this occasion it should find means so to inebriate any candid American as to make him forget what he owed to truth and to decency, or induce him either to believe or to say that the almost unanimous advice of the Convention proceeded from a wicked combination and conspiracy against the liberties of their country. This is not the temper with which we should receive and consider their recommendations, nor the treatment that would be worthy either of us or of them. Let us continue careful, therefore, that facts do not warrant historians to tell future generations that envy, malice, and uncharitableness pursued our patriotic benefactors to their graves, and that not even pre-eminence in virtue, nor lives devoted to the public, could shield them from obloquy and detraction. On the contrary, let our bosoms always retain a sufficient degree of honest indignation to disappoint and discourage those who expect our thanks or applause for calumniating our most faithful and meritorious friends. The Convention concurred in opinion with the people, that a national government, competent to every national object, was indispensably necessary; and it was as plain to them as it now is to all America, that the present Confederation does not provide for such a government. These points being agreed, they proceeded to consider how and in what manner such a government could be formed, as, on the one hand, should be sufficienty energetic to raise us from our prostrate and distressed situation, and, on the other, be perfectly consistent with the liberties of the people of every State. Like men to whom the experience of other ages and countries had taught wisdom, they not only determined that it should be erected by, and depend on, the people, but, remembering the many instances in which governments vested solely in one man, or one body of men, had degenerated into tyrannies, they judged it most prudent that the three great branches of power should be committed to different hands, and therefore that the executive should be separated from the legislative, and the judicial from both. Thus far the propriety of their work is easily seen and understood, and therefore is thus far almost universally approved; for no one man or thing under the sun ever yet pleased everybody.

The next question was, what particular powers should be given to these three branches. Here the different views and interests of the different States, as well as the different abstract opinions of their members on such points, interposed many difficulties. Here the business became complicated, and presented a wide field for investigation — too wide for every eye to take a quick and comprehensive view of it.

It is said that "in a multitude of counsellors there is safety," because, in the first place, there is greater security for probity; and in the next, if every member cast in only his mite of information and argument, their joint stock of both will thereby be greater than the stock possessed by any one single man out-of-doors. Gentlemen out-of-doors, therefore, should not be hasty in condemning a system which probably rests on more good reasons than they are aware of, especially when formed under such advantages, and recommended by so many men of distinguished worth and abilities.

The difficulties before mentioned occupied the Convention a long time; and it was not without mutual concessions that they were at last surmounted. These concessions serve to explain to us the reason why some parts of the system please in some States which displease in others, and why many of the objections which have been made to it are so contradictory and inconsistent with one another. It does great credit to the temper and talents of the Convention that they were able so to reconcile the different views and interests of the different States, and the clashing opinions of their members, as to unite with such singular and almost perfect unanimity in any plan whatever on a subject so intricate and perplexed. It shows that it must have been thoroughly discussed and understood; and probably if the community at large had the same lights and reasons before them they would, if equally candid and uninfluenced, be equally unanimous.

It would be arduous, and indeed impossible, to comprise within the limits of this address a full discussion of every part of the plan. Such a task would require a volume; and few men have leisure or inclination to read volumes on any subject. The objections made to it are almost without number, and many of them without reason. Some of them are real and honest, and others merely ostensible. There are friends to union and a national government who have serious doubts, who wish to be informed and to be convinced; and there are others who, neither wishing for union nor any national government at all, will oppose and object to any plan that can be contrived.

We are told, among other strange things, that the liberty of the press is left insecure by the proposed Constitution; and yet that Constitution says neither more nor less about it than the constitution of the State of New York does. We are told that it deprives us of trial by jury; whereas the fact is, that it expressly secures it in certain cases, and takes it away in none. It is absurd to construe the silence of this, or of our own constitution, relative to a great number of our rights, into a total extinction of them. Silence and blank paper neither grant nor take away anything. Complaints are also made that the proposed Constitution is not accompanied by a bill of rights; and yet they who make the complaints know, and are content, that no bill of rights accompanied the constitution of this State. In days and centuries when monarchs and their subjects were frequently disputing about prerogative and privileges, the latter then found it necessary, as it were, to run out the line between them, and oblige the former to admit, by solemn acts, called bills of rights, that certain enumerated rights belonged to the people, and were not comprehended in the royal prerogative. But, thank God, we have no such disputes; we have no monarchs to contend with or demand admissions from. The proposed government is to be the government of the people; all its officers are to be their officers, and to exercise no rights but such as the people commit to them. The Constitution serves only to point out that part of the people's business which they think proper by it to refer to the management of persons therein designated; those persons are to receive that business to manage, not for themselves and as their own, but as agents and overseers for the people, to whom they are constantly responsible, and by whom only they are to be appointed.

But the design of this address is not to investigate the merits of the plan, nor of the objections made to it. They who seriously contemplate the present state of our affairs will be convinced that other considerations, of at least equal importance demand their attention. Let it be admitted that this plan, like everything else devised by man, has its imperfections. That it does not please everybody, is certain; and there is little reason to expect one that will. It is a question of great moment to you, whether the probability of our being able seasonably to obtain a better, is such as to render it prudent or desirable to reject this and run the risk. Candidly to consider this question, is the design of this address.

As the importance of this question must be obvious to every man, whatever his private opinions may be, it becomes us all to treat it in that calm and temperate manner which a subject so deeply interesting to the future welfare of our country and propriety requires. Let us therefore, as much as possible, repress and compose that irritation in our minds which too warm disputes about it may have excited. Let us endeavor to forget that this or that man is on this or that side; and that we ourselves, perhaps without sufficient reflection, have classed ourselves with one or the other party. Let us remember that this is not a matter that only touches our local parties, but as one so great, so general, and so extensive, in its future consequence to America, that, for our deciding upon it according to the best of our unbiased judgment, we must be highly responsible both here and hereafter.

The question now before us naturally leads to three inquiries:

1. Whether it is probable that a better plan can be obtained.

2. Whether, if attainable, it is likely to be in season.

3. What would be our situation if, after rejecting this, all our efforts to obtain a better should prove fruitless.

The men who formed this plan are Americans, who had long deserved and enjoyed our confidence, and who are as much interested in having a good government as any of us are or can be. They were appointed to that business at a time when the States had become very sensible of the derangement of our national affairs and of the impossibility of retrieving them under the existing Confederation. Although well persuaded that nothing but a good national government could oppose and divert the tide of evils that were flowing in upon us, yet those gentlemen met in Convention with minds perfectly unprejudiced in favor of any particular plan. The minds of their constituents were at that time equally cool and dispassionate. All agreed in the necessity of doing something; but no one ventured to say decidedly what precisely ought to be done. Opinions were then fluctuating and unfixed; and whatever might have been the wishes of a few individuals, yet while the Convention deliberated the people remained in quiet suspense.

Neither wedded to favorite systems of their own, nor influenced by popular ones abroad, the members were more desirous to receive light from, than to impress their private sentiments on, one another.

These circumstances naturally opened the door to that spirit of candor, of calm inquiry, of mutual accommodation, and mutual respect which entered into the Convention with them and regulated their debates and proceedings.

The impossibility of agreeing upon any plan, that would exactly quadrate with the local policy and objects of every State, soon became evident; and they wisely thought it better mutually to coincide and accommodate, and in that way to fashion their system as much as possible by the circumstances and wishes of the different States, than by pertinaciously adhering each to his own ideas, oblige the Convention to rise without doing anything. They were sensible that obstacles, arising from local circumstances, would not cease while those circumstances continued to exist; and, so far as those circumstances depended on differences of climate, productions, and commerce, that no change was to be expected. They were likewise sensible that, on a subject so comprehensive and involving such a variety of points and questions, the most able, the most candid, and the most honest men will differ in opinion. The same proposition seldom strikes many minds in exactly the same point of light. Different habits of thinking, different degrees and modes of education, different prejudices and opinions, early formed and long entertained, conspire, with a multitude of other circumstances, to produce among men a diversity and contrariety of opinions on questions of difficulty. Liberality, therefore, as well as prudence, induced them to treat each other's opinions with tenderness, to argue without asperity, and to endeavor to convince the judgment without hurting the feelings of each other. Although many weeks were passed in these discussions, some points remained on which a unison of opinions could not be effected. Here, again, that same happy disposition to unite and conciliate induced them to meet each other; and enabled them, by mutual concessions, finally to complete and agree to the plan they have recommended, and that, too, with a degree of unanimity which, considering the variety of discordant views and ideas they had to reconcile, is really astonishing.

They tell us, very honestly, that this plan is the result of accommodation. They do not hold it up as the best of all possible ones, but only as the best which they could unite in and agree to. If such men, appointed and meeting under such auspicious circumstances, and so sincerely disposed to conciliation, could go no farther in their endeavors to please every State and every body, what reason have we, at present, to expect any system that would give more general satisfaction?

Suppose this plan to be rejected, what measures would you propose for obtaining a better? Some will answer: "Let us appoint another Convention; and, as everything has been said and written that can well be said and written on the subject, they will be better informed than the former one was, and consequently be better able to make and agree upon a more eligible one."

This reasoning is fair; and, as far as it goes, has weight; but it nevertheless takes one thing for granted which appears very doubtful; for, although the new Convention might have more information, and perhaps equal abilities, yet it does not from thence follow that they would be equally disposed to agree. The contrary of this position is most probable. You must have observed that the same temper and equanimity which prevailed among the people on former occasions no longer exist. We have unhappily become divided into parties, and this important subject has been handled with such indiscreet and offensive acrimony, and with so many little unhandsome artifices and misrepresentations, that pernicious heats and animosities have been kindled, and spread their flames far and wide among us. When, therefore, it becomes a question who shall be deputed to the new Convention, we cannot flatter ourselves that the talents and integrity of the candidates will determine who shall be elected. Federal electors will vote for federal deputies, and anti-federal electors for anti-federal ones. Nor will either party prefer the most moderate of their adherents; for, as the most staunch and active partisans will be the most popular, so the men most willing and able to carry points, to oppose and divide and embarrass their opponents, will be chosen. A Convention formed at such a season, and of such men, would be too exact an epitome of the great body that named them. The same party views, the same propensity to opposition, the same distrusts and jealousies, and the same unaccommodating spirit which prevail without, would be concentrated and ferment with still greater violence within. Each deputy would recollect who sent him, and why he was sent, and be too apt to consider himself bound in honor to contend and act vigorously under the standard of his party, and not to hazard their displeasure by preferring compromise to victory. As vice does not sow the seed of virtue, so neither does passion cultivate the fruits of reason. Suspicion and resentment create no disposition to conciliate, nor do they infuse a desire of making partial and personal objects bend to general union and common good. The utmost efforts of that excellent disposition were necessary to enable the late Convention to perform their task; and although contrary causes sometimes operate similar effects, yet to expect that discord and animosity should produce the fruits of confidence and agreement, is to expect "grapes from thorns and figs from thistles."

The States of Georgia, Delaware, Jersey, and Connecticut have adopted the present plan with unexampled unanimity. They are content with it as it is; and consequently their deputies, being apprised of the sentiments of their constituents, will be little inclined to make alterations, and cannot be otherwise than averse to changes which they have no reason to think would be acceptable to their people. Some other States, though less unanimous, have nevertheless adopted it by very respectable majorities, and for reasons so evidently cogent that even the minority in one of them have nobly pledged themselves for its promotion and support. From these circumstances the new Convention would derive and experience difficulties unknown to the former. Nor are these the only additional difficulties they would have to encounter. Few are ignorant that there has lately sprung up a set of politicians who teach, and profess to believe, that the extent of our nation is too great for the superintendence of one national government, and on that principle agree that it ought to be divided into two or three. This doctrine, however mischievous in its tendency and consequences, has its advocates; and should any of them be sent to the Convention, it will be naturally their policy rather to cherish than to prevent divisions; for, well knowing that the institution of any national government would, blast their favorite system, no measures that lead to it can meet with their aid or approbation.

Nor can we be certain whether or not any and what, foreign influence would, on such an occasion, be indirectly exerted, nor for what purposes. Delicacy forbids an ample discussion of this question. Thus much may be said without error or offence, viz.: that such foreign nations as desire the prosperity of America, would rejoice to see her become great and powerful, under the auspices of a government wisely calculated to extend her commerce, to encourage her navigation and marine, and to direct the whole weight of her power and resources as her interest and honor may require, will doubtless be friendly to the union of States, and to the establishment of a government able to perpetuate, protect, and dignify it. Such other foreign nations, if any such there be, jealous of our growing importance, and fearful that our commerce and navigation should impair their own, behold our rapid population with regret, and apprehend that the enterprising spirit of our people, when seconded by power and probability of success, may be directed to objects not consistent with their policy or interests, cannot fail to wish that we may continue a weak and a divided people.

These considerations merit much attention; and candid men will judge how far they render it probable that a new Convention would be able either to agree in a better plan, or, with tolerable unanimity, in any plan at all. Any plan, forcibly carried by a slender majority, must expect numerous opponents among the people, who, especially in their present temper, would be more inclined to reject than adopt any system so made and carried. We should, in such a case, again see the press teeming with publications for and against it; for, as the minority would take pains to justify their dissent, so would the majority be industrious to display the wisdom of their proceeding. Hence new divisions, new parties, and new distractions would ensue; and no one can foresee or conjecture when or how they would terminate.

Let those who are sanguine in their expectations of a better plan from a new Convention, also reflect on the delays and risks to which it would expose us. Let them consider whether we ought, by continuing much longer in our present humiliating condition, to give other nations further time to perfect their restrictive systems of commerce, reconcile their own people to them, and to fence, and guard, and strengthen them by all those regulations and contrivances in which a jealous policy is ever fruitful. Let them consider whether we ought to give further opportunities to discord to alienate the hearts of our citizens from one another, and thereby encourage new Cromwells to bold exploits. Are we certain that our foreign creditors will continue patient, and ready to proportion their forbearance to our delays? Are we sure that our distresses, dissensions, and weakness will neither invite hostility nor insult? If they should, how ill prepared shall we be for defence, without union, without government, without money, and without credit!

It seems necessary to remind you that some time must yet elapse before all the States will have decided on the present plan. If they reject it, some time must also pass before the measure of a new Convention can be brought about and generally agreed to. A further space of time will then be requisite to elect their deputies, and send them on to Convention. What time they may expend, when met, cannot be divined; and it is equally uncertain how much time the several States may take to deliberate and decide on any plan they may recommend. If adopted, still a further space of time will be necessary to organize and set it in motion. In the meantime, our affairs are daily going from bad to worse; and it is not rash to say that our distresses are accumulating like compound interest.

But if, for reasons already mentioned, and others that we cannot now perceive, the new Convention, instead of producing a better plan, should give us only a history of our disputes, or should offer us one still less pleasing than the present, where should we be? Then the old Confederation has done its best, and cannot help us; and is now so relaxed and feeble, that, in all probability, it would not survive so violent a shock.

Then "To your tents, O Israel!" would be the word. Then every band of union would be severed. Then every State would be a little nation, jealous of its neighbor, and anxious to strengthen itself, by foreign alliances, against its former friends. Then farewell to fraternal affection, unsuspecting intercourse, and mutual participation in commerce, navigation, and citizenship. Then would rise mutual restrictions and fears, mutual garrisons and standing armies, and all those dreadful evils which for so many ages plagued England, Scotland, Wales, and Ireland, while they continued disunited, and were played off against each other.

Consider, my fellow-citizens, what you are about before it is too late; consider what in such an event would be your particular case. You know the geography of your State, and the consequences of your local position. Jersey and Connecticut, to whom your impost laws have been unkind—Jersey and Connecticut, who have adopted the present plan and expect much good from it, will impute its miscarriage and all the consequent evils to you. They now consider your opposition as dictated more by your fondness for your impost, than for those rights to which they have never been behind you in attachment. They cannot, they will not, love you; they border upon you and are your neighbors, but you will soon cease to regard their neighborhood as a blessing. You have but one port or outlet to your commerce, and how you are to keep that outlet free and uninterrupted merits consideration. What advantages Vermont, in combination with others, might take of you, may easily be conjectured; nor will you be at a loss to perceive how much reason the people of Long Island, whom you cannot protect, have to deprecate being constantly exposed to the depredations of every invader.

These are short hints; they ought not to be more developed; you can easily in your own minds dilate and trace them through all their relative circumstances and connections. Pause then for a moment and reflect whether the matters you are disputing about are of sufficient moment to justify your running such extravagant risks. Reflect that the present plan comes recommended to you by men and fellow-citizens who have given you the highest proofs that men can give, of their justice, their love of liberty and their country, of their prudence, of their application, and of their talents. They tell you it is the best that they could form, and that in their opinion, it is necessary to redeem you from those calamities which already begin to be heavy upon us all. You find that not only those men, but others of similar characters, and of whom you have also had very ample experience, advise you to adopt it. You find that whole States concur in the sentiment, and among them are your next neighbors, both of whom have shed much blood in the cause of liberty, and have manifested as strong and constant a predilection for a free republican government as any States in the Union, and perhaps in the world. They perceive not those latent mischiefs in it with which some double-sighted politicians endeavor to alarm you. You cannot but be sensible that this plan or Constitution will always be in the hands and power of the people, and that if on experiment it should be found defective or incompetent, they may either remedy its defects, or substitute another in its room. The objectionable parts of it are certainly very questionable, for otherwise there would not be such a contrariety of opinions about them. Experience will better determine such questions than theoretical arguments, and so far as the danger of abuses is urged against the institution of a government, remember that a power to do good always involves a power to do harm. We must, in the business of government as well as in all other business, have some degree of confidence, as well as a great degree of caution. Who, on a sick-bed, would refuse medicines from a physician merely because it is as much in his power to administer deadly poisons as salutary remedies?

You cannot be certain that by rejecting the proposed plan you would not place yourselves in a very awkward situation. Suppose nine States should nevertheless adopt it, would you not in that case be obliged either to separate from the Union or rescind your dissent? The first would not be eligible, nor could the latter be pleasant. A mere hint is sufficient on this topic. You cannot but be aware of the consequences.

Consider, then, how weighty and how many considerations advise and persuade the people of America to remain in the safe and easy path of union; to continue to move and act, as they hitherto have done, as a band of brothers; and to have confidence in themselves and in one another; and, since all cannot see with the same eyes, at least to give the proposed Constitution a fair trial, and to mend it as time, occasion, and experience may dictate. It would little become us to verify the predictions of those who ventured to prophesy that peace, instead of blessing us with happiness and tranquillity, would serve only as the signal for factions, discord, and civil contentions to rage in our land, and overwhelm it with misery and distress.

Let us all be mindful that the cause of freedom depends on the use we make of the singular opportunities we enjoy of governing ourselves wisely; for, if the event should prove that the people of this country either cannot or will not govern themselves, who will hereafter be advocates for systems which, however charming in theory and prospect, are not reducible to practice? If the people of our nation, instead of consenting to be governed by laws of their own making and rulers of their own choosing, should let licentiousness, disorder, and confusion reign over them, the minds of men everywhere will insensibly become alienated from republican forms, and prepared to prefer and acquiesce in governments which, though less friendly to liberty, afford more peace and security.

Receive this address with the same candor with which it is written; and may the spirit of wisdom and patriotism direct and distinguish your councils and your conduct.

A Citizen of New York.

PRESIDENT WASHINGTON TO JAY.
New York, 5th October, 1789

Sir,

It is with singular pleasure that I address you as Chief Justice of the Supreme Court of the United States, for which office your commission is enclosed.

In nominating you for the important Station, which you now fill, I not only acted in conformity to my best judgment, but I trust I did a grateful thing to the good citizens of these United States; and I have a full Confidence that the love which you bear to our country, and a desire to promote the general happiness, will not suffer you to hesitate a moment to bring into action the talents, knowledge, and integrity which are so necessary to be exercised at the head of that department which must be considered as the keystone of our political fabric.

I have the honor to be, with high consideration and sentiments of esteem, &c.,

Geo. Washington.

JAY TO PRESIDENT WASHINGTON.
New York, October 6, 1789

Sir:

When distinguished discernment and patriotism unite in selecting men for stations of trust and dignity, they derive honor not only from their offices, but from the hand which confers them.

With a mind and a heart impressed with these re ec-tions, and their correspondent sensations, I assure you that the sentiments expressed in your letter of yesterday and implied by the commission it enclosed, will never cease to excite my best endeavors to ful l the duties imposed by the latter, and as far as may be in my power, to realize the expectations which your nominations, especially to impor-tant places, must naturally create.

With the most perfect respect, esteem, and attach-ment I have the honor to be, sir,

Your most obedient and humble servant,
John Jay

CHARGE TO GRAND JURIES
BY CHIEF-JUSTICE JAY

Whether any people can long govern themselves in an equal, uniform, and orderly manner, is a question which the advocates for free government justly consider as being exceedingly important to the cause of liberty. This question, like others whose solution depends on facts, can only be determined by experience. It is a question on which many think some room for doubt still remains. Men have had very few fair opportunities of making the experiment; and this is one reason why less progress has been made in the science of government than in almost any other. The far greater number of the constitutions and governments of which we are informed have originated in force or in fraud, having been either imposed by improper exertions of power, or introduced by the arts of designing individuals, whose apparent zeal for liberty and the public good enabled them to take advantage of the credulity and misplaced confidence of their fellow-citizens.

Providence has been pleased to bless the people of this country with more perfect opportunities of choosing, and more effectual means of establishing their own government, than any other nation has hitherto enjoyed; and for the use we may make of these opportunities and of these means we shall be highly responsible to that Providence, as well as to mankind in general, and to our own posterity in particular. Our deliberations and proceedings being unawed and uninfluenced by power or corruption, domestic or foreign, are perfectly free; our citizens are generally and greatly enlightened, and our country is so extensive that the personal influence of popular individuals can rarely embrace large portions of it. The institution of general and State governments, their respective conveniences and defects in practice, and the subsequent alterations made in some of them, have operated as useful experiments, and conspired to promote our advancement in this interesting science. It is pleasing to observe that the present national government already affords advantages which the preceding one proved too feeble and ill-constructed to produce. How far it may be still distant from the degree of perfection to which it may possibly be carried, time only can decide. It is a consolation to re ect that the good-sense of the people will be enabled by experience to discover and correct its imperfections, especially while they continue to retain a proper confidence in themselves, and avoid those jealousies and dissensions which, often springing from the worst designs, frequently frustrate the best measures.

Wise and virtuous men have thought and reasoned very differently respecting government, but in this they have at length very unanimously agreed, viz., that its powers should be divided into three distinct, independent departments—the executive, legislative and judicial. But how to constitute and balance them in such a manner as best to guard against abuse and uctuation, and preserve the Constitution from encroachments, are points on which there continues to be a great diversity of opinions, and on which we have all as yet much to learn. The Constitution of the United States has accordingly instituted these three departments, and much pains have been taken so to form and de ne them as that they may operate as checks one upon the other, and keep each within its proper limits; it being universally agreed to be of the last importance to a free people, that they who are vested with executive, legislative, and judicial powers should rest satis ed with their respective portions of power, and neither encroach on the provinces of each other, nor suffer themselves to intermeddle with the rights reserved by the Constitution to the people. If, then, so much depends on our rightly improving the before-mentioned opportunities, if the most discerning and enlightened minds may be mistaken relative to theories unconfirmed by practice, if on such difficult questions men may differ in opinion and yet be patriots, and if the merits of our opinions can only be ascertained by experience, let us patiently abide the trial, and unite our endeavors to render it a fair and an impartial one.

These remarks may not appear very pertinent to the present occasion, and yet it will be readily admitted that occasions of promoting good-will, and good-temper, and the progress of useful truths among our fellow-citizens should not be omitted. These motives urge me further to observe, that a variety of local and other circumstances rendered the formation of the judicial department particularly difficult.

We had become a nation. As such we were responsible to others for the observance of the Laws of Nations; and as our national concerns were to be regulated by national laws, national tribunals became necessary for the interpretation and execution of them both. No tribunals of the like kind and extent had heretofore existed in this country. From such, therefore, no light of experience nor facilities of usage and habit were to be derived. Our jurisprudence varied in almost every State, and was accommodated to local, not general convenience; to partial, not national policy. This convenience and this policy were nevertheless to be regarded and tenderly treated. A judicial controul, general and final, was indispensable; the manner of establishing it with powers neither too extensive nor too limited, rendering it properly independent, and yet properly amenable, involved questions of no little intricacy.

The expediency of carrying justice, as it were, to every man's door, was obvious; but how to do it in an expedient manner was far from being apparent. To provide against discord between national and State jurisdictions, to renderthem auxiliary instead of hostile to each other, and so to connect both as to leave each sufficiently independent, and yet sufficiently combined, was and will be arduous.

Institutions formed under such circumstances should therefore be received with candor and tried with temper and prudence. It was under these embarrassing circumstances that the articles in the Constitution on this subject, as well as the act of Congress for establishing the judicial courts of the United States were made and passed. Under the authority of that act, this court now sits. Its jurisdiction is twofold, civil and criminal. To the exercise of the latter you, gentlemen, are necessary, and for that purpose are now convened.

The most perfect constitutions, the best governments, and the wisest laws are vain, unless well administered and well obeyed. Virtuous citizens will observe them from a sense of duty, but those of an opposite description can be restrained only by fear of disgrace and punishment. Such being the state of things, it is essential to the welfare of society, and to the protection of each member of it in the peaceable enjoyment of his rights, that offenders be punished. The end of punishment, however, is not to expiate for offences, but by the terror of example to deter men from the commission of them. To render these examples useful, policy as well as morality requires not only that punishment be proportionate to guilt, but that all proceedings against persons accused or suspected, should be accompanied by the re ectionthat they may be innocent. Hence, therefore, it is proper that dispassionate and careful inquiry should precede these rigors which justice exacts, and which should always be tempered with as much humanity and benevolence as the nature of such cases may admit. Warm, partial, and precipitate prosecutions, and cruel and abominable executions, such as racks, embowelling, drawing, quartering, burning and the like, are no less impolitic than inhuman; they infuse into the public mind disgust at the barbarous severity of government, and fill it with pity and partiality for the sufferers. On the contrary, when offenders are prosecuted with temper and decency, when they are convicted after impartial trials, and punished in a manner becoming the dignity of public justice to prescribe, the feelings and sentiments of men will be on the side of government; and however disposed they may and ought to be, to regard suffering offenders with compassion, yet that compassion will never be unmixed with a due degree of indignation. We are happy that the genius of our laws is mild, and we have abundant reason to rejoice in possessing one of the best institutions that ever was devised for bringing offenders to justice without endangering the peace and security of the innocent. I mean that of Grand Juries. Greatly does it tend to promote order and good government that in every district there should frequently be assembled a number of the most discreet and respectable citizens in it, who on their oaths are bound to inquire into and present all offences committed against the laws in such districts, and greatly does it tend to the quiet and safety of good and peaceful citizens, that no man can be put in jeopardy for imputed crimes without such previous inquiry and presentment.

The extent of your district, gentlemen, which is commensurate with the State, necessarily extends your duty throughout every county in it, and demands proportionate diligence in your inquiries and circumspection in your presentments. The objects of your inquiry are all offences committed against the laws of the United States in this district, or on the high seas, by persons now in the district. You will recollect that the laws of nations make part of the laws of this and of every other civilized nation. They consist of those rules for regulating the conduct of nations towards each other which, resulting from right reason, receive their obligations from that principle and from general assent and practice. To this head also belong those rules or laws which by agreement become established between particular nations, and of this kind are treaties, conventions, and the like compacts; as in private life a fair and legal contract between two men cannot be annulled nor altered by either without the consent of the other, so neither can treaties between nations. States and legislatures may repeal their regulating statutes, but they cannot repeal their bargains. Hence it is that treaties fairly made and concluded are perfectly obligatory, and ought to be punctually observed. We are now a nation, and it equally becomes us to perform our duties as to assert our rights. The penal statutes of the United States are few, and principally respect the revenue. The right ordering and management of this important business is very essential to the credit, character, and prosperity of our country. On the citizens at large is placed the burthen of providing for the public exigencies; whoever, therefore, fraudulently withdraws his shoulder from that common burthen necessarily leaves his portion of the weight to be borne by the others, and thereby does injustice not only to the government but to them.

Direct your attention also to the conduct of the national of cers, and let not any corruptions, frauds, extortions, or criminal negligences, with which you may nd any of them justly chargeable, pass unnoticed. In a word, gentlemen, your province and your duty extend (as has been before observed) to the inquiry and presentment of all offences of every kind committed against the United States in this district or on the high seas by persons in it. If in the performance of your duty you should meet with difficulties, the court will be ready to afford you proper assistance.

It cannot be too strongly impressed on the minds of us all how greatly our individual prosperity depends on our national prosperity, and how greatly our national prosperity depends on a well organized, vigorous government, ruling by wise and equal laws, faithfully executed; nor is such a government unfriendly to liberty—to that liberty which is really inestimable; on the contrary, nothing but a strong government of laws irresistibly bearing down arbitrary power and licentiousness can defend it against those two formidable enemies. Let it be remembered that civil liberty consists not in a right to every man to do just what he pleases, but it consists in an equal right to all the citizens to have, enjoy, and to do, in peace, security, and without molestation, whatever the equal and constitutional laws of the country admit to be consistent with the public good. It is the duty and the interest, therefore, of all good citizens, in their several stations, to support the laws and the government which thus protect their rights and liberties.

I am persuaded, gentlemen, that you will cheerfully and faithfully perform the task now assigned you, and I forbear, by additional remarks, to detain you longer from it.

May 4th, 1790
John Jay

REPLY OF NEW YORK JURY
TO CHIEF-JUSTICE JAY

May it please your Honors:

The very Excellent Charge given to the Grand Jury of this District by his Honor the Chief Judge of the Federal Court, demands our thanks and particular attention; and that it may be more in uential and impress the mind of our fellow citizens at large beg leave to ask a Copy of it for the press. Your Honors may be assured we shall in our several departments when dismissed exert our influence to promote peace, good order, and a strict regard to the laws of the United States agreeably to the Constitution so lately adopted; and we trust the judicial department will ever be lled, as it now is, with gentlemen of the first characters for learning, integrity, and ability.

We wish your Honors the Divine presence in all your circuits, and that you may be continually guarded by a good Providence.

Benj. Austin, Foreman.
May 4th, 1790.

PRESIDENT WASHINGTON TO THE "CHIEF JUSTICE AND ASSOCIATE JUSTICES OF THE SUPREME COURT OF THE UNITED STATES."

United States, April 3, 1790.

Gentlemen,

I have always been persuaded that the stability and success of the national government, and consequently the happiness of the people of the United States, would depend in a considerable degree on the interpretation and execution of its laws. In my opinion, therefore, it is important that the Judiciary system should not only be independent in its operations, but as perfect as possible in its formation.

As you are about to commence your first circuit, and many things may occur in such an unexplored field, which it would be useful should be known, I think it proper to acquaint you, that it will be agreeable to me to receive such information and remarks on this subject as you shall from time to time judge expedient to communicate.

G. Washington.

ALEXANDER HAMILTON TO JAY

My dear Sir,

I enclose you copies of two resolutions which have passed the house of representatives of Virginia. Others had been proposed and disagreed to; but the war was still going on. A spirited remonstrance to Congress is talked of.

This is the first symptom of a spirit which must either be killed or will kill the Constitution of the United States. I send the resolutions to you that it may be considered what ought to be done. Ought not the collective weight of the different parts of the Government to be employed in exploding the principles they contain? This question arises out of a sudden and un edged thought.

I remain, Dear Sir,

Your Affectionate and Obedient humble Servant,

A. Hamilton.

"Resolved, that so much of the act, entitled an act making provision for the debt of the United States, as limits the right of the United States in their redemption of the public debt is dangerous to the rights and subversive of the interest of the people, and demands the marked disapprobation of the General Assembly."

"Resolved, that it is the opinion of this Committee, that so much of the act of Congress, entitled 'an act making provision for the debt of the United States,' as assumes the payment of the state debt is repugnant to the Constitution of the United States, as it goes to the exercise of a power not expressly granted to the general government."

JAY TO PRESIDENT WASHINGTON
Boston, 13th November, 1790

Dear Sir:

The act "to regulate trade and intercourse with the Indian tribes," passed the last session, directs that the superintendents and persons by them licensed, shall be governed, in all things touching the said trade and intercourse, by such rules and regulations as the President shall prescribe. I was lately asked, Whether any and what arrangements had been made in pursuance of this act? My answer was, that I had not heard, but was persuaded that every thing necessary either had been or would soon be done. As every licensed trader must know what rules and regulations he is to obey and observe, would it be amiss to publish them?

The Constitution gives power to the Congress "to coin money, regulate the value thereof, and of foreign coin; to provide for the punishment of counterfeiting the securities and current coin of the United States." If the word current had been omitted, it might have been doubted whether the Congress could have punished the counterfeiting of foreign coin. Mexican dollars have long been known in our public acts as current coin. The 55th section of the act "to provide more effectually for the collection of the duties," etc., enumerates a variety of foreign coins which shall be received for the duties and fees mentioned in it.

The late penal act (as it is generally called) provides punishment for counterfeiting paper, but not coin, foreign or domestic. Whether this omission was accidental or designed, I am uninformed. It appears to me more expedient that this offence, as it respects current coin, should be punished in a uniform manner throughout the nation, rather than be left to State laws and State courts.

The Constitution provides, that "no State shall coin money, nor make any thing but gold or silver coin a tender in payment of debts." Must not this gold and silver coin be such only as shall be either struck or made current by the Congress? At present, I do not recollect any act which designates, unless perhaps by implication, what coins shall be a legal tender between citizen and citizen.

The Congress have power to establish post roads. This would be nugatory unless it implied a power either to repair these roads themselves, or compel others to do it. The former seems to be the more natural construction. Possibly the turnpike plan might gradually and usefully be introduced.

It appears advisable that the United States should have a fortress near the heads of the western waters; perhaps at, or not very distant from, Fort Pitt, to secure the communication between the western and Atlantic countries, and that the place be such as would cover the building of vessels proper for the navigation of the most important of those waters. Should not West Point, or a better post if it be found on Hudson River, be kept up? An impregnable harbor in the north, and another in the south, seem to me very desirable. Peace is the time to prepare for defence against hostilities.

There is some reason to apprehend that masts and ship-timber will, as cultivation advances, become scarce, unless some measures be taken to prevent their waste, or provide for the preservation of a sufficient fund of both.

Being persuaded that we could undersell other nations in salted provisions, especially beef, porvided none but of the first quality was exported, I am inclined to think the national government should attend to it; nay, that the whole business of inspecting all such of our exports of every kind as may be thought to require inspection, should be done under their exclusive authority, in a uniform manner. Where State inspection laws are good they might be adopted. If the individual States inspect by different rules, and some of them not at all, the article in question will not go to market with such plain and decided evidence of quality as to merit confidence, especially as various marks under various State laws multiply the means of fraud and imposition; if only the best commodities in their kind were exported, we should gain in name and price what we might lose at first by diminution of quality.

I think it probable that this letter will nd you at Philadelphia; if not, I presume it will be forwarded by some of your family, but how, or by whom, is uncertain. Much content and good-humor is observable in these States. The acts of Congress are as well respected and observed as could have been expected. The assumption gives general satisfaction here. The deviation from contract respecting interest is censured by some. They say, and not without reason, that the application of surplus revenue to the purchase of stock shows that the measure did not result from necessity.

With the most perfect respect, esteem, and attachment, I have the honor to be, dear sir,

Your obliged and obedient servant,
John Jay.

PRESIDENT WASHINGTON TO JAY
Mount Vernon, Nov. 19th, 1790

My Dear Sir,

The day is near when Congress is to commence its third session; and on Monday next, nothing intervening to prevent it, I shall set out to meet them at their new residence.

If any thing in the judiciary line, if any thing of a more general nature, proper for me to communicate to that body at the opening of the session, has occurred to you, you would oblige me by submitting them with the freedom and frankness of friendship.

The length and badness of the road from hence to Philadelphia, added to the unsettled weather which may be expected at this season, will more than probable render the term of my arrival at that place uncertain; but your sentiments, under cover, lodged with Mr. Lear by the first of next month, will be in time to meet me and the communications from the other great departments; and with such matters as have been handed immediately to myself from other quarters, or which have come under my own observation and contemplation during the recess, will enable me to form the sum of my communications to Congress at the opening of the session.

I shall say nothing of domestic occurrences in this letter, and those of foreign import you would receive at second-hand from hence. To add assurances of my friendship and regard would not be new; but with truth I can declare that I am

Your affectionate and humble servant,
George Washington

JAY TO ALEXANDER HAMILTON
Boston, 28th November, 1790

Dear Sir:

On returning from Exeter the evening before the last, I had the pleasure of receiving your letter of the 13th instant with the two copies mentioned in it. Having no apprehension of such measures, what was to be done appeared to me to be a question of some difficulty.as well as importance; to treat them as very important might render them more so than I think they are. The author of "McFingall" could do justice to the subject. The assumption will do its own work; it will justify itself and not want advocates. Every indecent interference of State assemblies will diminish their influence; the national government has only to do what is right and, if possible, be silent. If compelled to speak, it should be in few words strongly evinced of temper, dignity, and self-respect. Conversation and desultory paragraphs will do the rest.

Conversing to-day with General Lincoln I nd he doubts the expediency of some provision in the proposed act respecting the coasting trade, etc. He seems well informed about these matters. It struck me, and I observed, that his passing a few days at Philadelphia and conversing with you might be useful. I believe he wishes it; considering the season, he thinks no inconvenience would result from his being absent a little while from his station. If you should think it best to send him leave of absence now, he could immediately set out. I told him I should mention this much to you. I often hear his conduct commended, and I really believe with reason.

I have heard it suggested that a revenue officer shouldbe stationed on the communication with Canada. The facility of introducing valuable goods by that route is obvious. The national government gains ground in these countries, and I hope care will be taken to cherish the national spirit which is prevailing in them. The deviation from contract touching interest does not please very universally.

Yours affectionately,
John Jay

NEW YORK COMMITTEE TO JAY
To the Honorable John Jay, Esquire,
Chief Justice of the United States:

Sir:

Permit us in behalf of ourselves and the very respectable body of our fellow citizens, which we have the honor to represent, to congratulate you upon your safe return to this City from the Eastern Circuit.

The friends of liberty have ever entertained a lively sense of the important services which you have rendered to your country in every situation in which you have been placed. Whether they examine your conduct as a Member of the General Congress at the most trying periods of the late war, and of the Convention which framed the Constitution of this State, or consider your agency in negotiating the treaty which secured to America the blessings of peace, liberty and safety—they nd a continued display of abilities and virtue which will hand your name down to remote posterity as one of the illustrious defenders of the rights of Man.

It was this sense, Sir, of your public services which induced the independent freeholders of the State to nominate and support you at the last election as a candidate for the of ce of their Chief Magistrate, and procured you a decided majority of votes. Thus called to enjoy one of the highest honors in the power of a grateful people to bestow, it was not to be expected that you would have been deprived of it by the machinations of a few interested and designing men. In contempt, however, of the sacred voice of the people, in de ance of the Constitution, and in violation of uniform practice and the settled principles of law, we have seen a majority of the canvassing Committee reject the votes of whole Counties for the purpose of excluding

74

you and making way for a Governor of their own choice. This wanton and daring attack upon the invaluable rights of suffrage has excited a serious alarm amongst the electors of the State, and united them in measures to obtain redress. In the pursuit of an object so interesting we shall like freemen act with moderation and order; but at the same time with zeal and perseverance. Whilst we respect the laws, we respect ourselves and our rights and feel the strongest obligations to assert and maintain them. The cause in which we are engaged being the cause of the people we trust that it cannot fail of success; but in every event we entreat you to believe that you will retain a distinguished place in our affections, and that we shall embrace every opportunity to manifest the unbounded confidence which we repose in your talents and patriotism.

By order of the Committee,
Nicholas Cruger, Chairman. New York, July 13th, 1792.

JAY'S REPLY
TO THE NEW YORK COMMITTEE

Gentlemen:

It is far more pleasing to receive proofs of the confidence and attachment of my native city than it is easy to express the sense which that confidence and that attachment inspire. When I re ect on the sacri ces and efforts in the cause of liberty, which distinguished this State during the late war, my feelings are very sensibly affected by the favorable light in which you regard my conduct during that interesting period. That cause was patronized by Him who gave to men the rights we claimed. He crowned it with success, and made it instrumental to our enjoying a degree of national prosperity unknown to any other people. May it be perpetual! Such is our Constitution, and such are the means of preserving order and good government, with which we are blessed, that, while our citizens remain virtuous, free, and enlightened, few political evils can occur, for which remedies perfectly effectual, and yet perfectly consistent with general tranquillity, cannot be found and applied.

I derive great satisfaction from the hope and expectation that the event which at present excites so much alarm and anxiety, will give occasion only to such measures as patriotism may direct and justify; and that the vigilance and wisdom of the people will always afford to their rights that protection for which other countries, less informed, have often too precipitately recurred to violence and commotion.

In questions touching our constitutional privileges, all the citizens are equally interested; and the social duties call upon us to unite in discussing those questions with candor and temper, in deciding them with circumspection and impartiality, and in maintaining the equal rights of all withconstancy and fortitude.

They who do what they have a right to do, give no just cause of offence; and therefore every consideration of propriety forbids that differences in opinion respecting candidates should suspend or interrupt that mutual good-humor and benevolence which harmonizes society, and softens the asperities incident to human life and human affairs.

By those free and independent electors who have given me their suffrages. I esteem myself honored; for the virtuous, who withheld that mark of preference, I retain, and ought to retain, my former respect and good-will. To all I wish prosperity, public and private. Permit me, gentlemen, to assure you and your constituents that, as I value their esteem, and rejoice in their approbation, so it will always be my desire, as well as my duty, to justify as far as possible the sentiments which they entertain of me, and which you, sir, have expressed in terms and in a manner which demand and which receive my warmest acknowledgments.

ALEXANDER HAMILTON TO JAY
Philadelphia, December 18th, 1792.

My dear Sir:

Your favors of the 26th November and 16th inst. have duly come to hand. I am ashamed that the former has remained so long unacknowledged; though I am persuaded my friends would readily excuse my delinquencies, could they appreciate my situation. 'Tis not the load of proper of cial business that alone engrosses me, though this would be enough to occupy any man. 'Tis not the extra attentions I am obliged to pay to the course of legislative manœuvres, that alone adds to my burthen and perplexity. 'Tis the malicious intrigues to stab me in the dark, against which I am too often obliged to guard myself, that distract and harass me to a point, which, rendering my situation scarcely tolerable, interferes with objects to which friendship and inclination would prompt me.

I have not, however, been unmindful of the subject of your letters. Mr. King will tell you the state the business was in. Nothing material has happened since. The representation will probably produce some effect, though not as great as ought to be expected. Some changes for the better, I trust, will take place.

The success of the vice-president is as great a source of satisfaction, as that of Mr. Clinton would have been of morti cation and pain to me. Willingly, however, would I relinquish my share of the command to the anti-federalists, if I thought they were to be trusted. But I have so many proofs of the contrary, as to make me dread the experiment of their preponderance.

Very respecttully and affectionately, dear sir, Your obedient servant, A. Hamilton

JAY TO ALEXANDER HAMILTON.
New York, 29th December, 1792

Dear Sir:

On my return this evening from Rye, I found your letter of the 18th instant at my house. It is not difficult to perceive that your situation is unpleasant, and it is easy to predict that your enemies will endeavor to render it still more so. The thorns they strew in your way will (if you please) hereafter blossom, and furnish garlands to decorate your administration. Resolve not to be driven from your station, and as your situation must, it seems, be militant, act accordingly. Envy will tell posterity that your difficulties, from the state of things, were inconsiderable, compared with the great, growing, and untouched resources of the nation. Your difficulties from persons and party will, by time, be carried out of sight, unless you prevent it. No other person will possess sufficient facts and details to do full justice to the subject, and I think your reputation points to the expediency of memoirs. You want time, it is true, but few of us know how much time we can find when we set about it.

Had not your letter come from the post-office, I should suspect it had been opened. The wafer looked very much like it. Such letters should be sealed with wax, impressed with your seal.

I rejoice with you in the re-election of Mr. Adams. It has relieved my mind from much inquietude. It is a great point gained; but the unceasing industry and arts of the Anties render perseverance, union, and constant efforts necessary. Adieu, my dear sir.

Yours sincerely,
John Jay.

OPINION OF CHIEF-JUSTICE JAY
ON THE SUABILITY OF A STATE

The question we are now to decide has been accurately stated, viz.: Is a State suable by individual citizens of another State?

It is said that Georgia refuses to appear and answer to the plaintiff in this action, because she is a sovereign State, and therefore not liable to such actions. In order to ascertain the merits of this objection, let us inquire — first, in what sense Georgia is a sovereign State; second, whether suability is incompatible with such sovereignty; third, whether the Constitution, to which Georgia is a party, authorizes such an action against her.

Suability and suable are words not in common use, but they concisely and correctly convey the idea annexed to them.

First, in determining the sense in which Georgia is a sovereign State, it may be useful to turn our attention to the political situation we were in prior to the Revolution, and to the political rights which emerged from the Revolution. All the country now possessed by the United States was then a part of the dominions appertaining to the crown of Great Britain. Every acre of land in this country was then held, mediately or immediately, by grants from that crown. All the people of this country were then subjects of the King of Great Britain, and owed allegiance to him, and all the civil authority then existing or exercised here owed from the head of the British Empire. They were in strict sense fellow-subjects, and in a variety of respects one people. When the Revolution commenced, the patriots did not assert that only the same af nity and social connection subsisted between the people of the Colonies which subsisted between the people of Gaul, Britain, and

Spain, while Roman provinces, — viz., only that affinity and social connection which result from the mere circumstance of being governed by the same prince. Different ideas prevailed, and gave occasion to the Congress of 1774 and 1775.

The Revolution, or rather the Declaration of Independence, found the people already united for general purposes, and at the same time providing for their more domestic concerns, by State conventions and other temporary arrangements. From the crown of Great Britain the sovereignty of their country passed to the people of it; and it was then not an uncommon opinion that the unappropriated lands, which belonged to that crown, passed not to the people of the Colony or States within whose limits they were situated, but to the whole people. On whatever principles this opinion rested, it did not give way to the other; and thirteen sovereignties were considered as emerged from the principles of the Revolution, combined with local convenience and considerations. The people, nevertheless, continued to consider themselves, in a national point of view, as one people; and they continued, without interruption, to manage their national concerns accordingly. Afterwards, in the hurry of the war, and in the warmth of mutual confidence, they made a confederation of the States the basis of a general government. Experience disappointed the expectations they had formed from it; and then the people, in their collective and national capacity, established the present Constitution. It is remarkable that, in establishing it, the people exercised their own rights and their own proper sovereignty; and, conscious of the plentitude of it, they declared, with becoming dignity: "We, the people of the United States, do ordain and establish this Constitution." Here we see the people acting as sovereigns of the whole country, and, in the language of sovereignty, establishing a Constitution, by which it was their will that the State governments should be bound, and to which the State constitutions should be made to conform. Every

State constitution is a compact made by and between the citizens of a State to govern themselves in a certain manner; and the Constitution of the United States is likewise a compact made by the people of the United States to govern themselves as to general objects in a certain manner. By this great compact, however, many prerogatives were transferred to the national government, such as those of making war and peace, contracting alliances, coining money, etc., etc.

If then it be true, that the sovereignty of the nation is in the people of the nation, and the residuary sovereignty of each State in the people of each State, it may be useful to compare these sovereignties with those in Europe, that we may thence be enabled to judge, whether all the prerogatives which are allowed to the latter, are so essential to the former. There is reason to suspect that some of the dificulties which embarrass the present question, arise from inattention to differences which subsist between them.

It will be sufficient to observe, briefly, that the sovereignties in Europe, and particularly in England, exist on feudal principles. That system considers the prince as the sovereign, and the people as his subjects; it regards his person as the object of allegiance, and excludes the idea of his being on an equal footing with a subject, either in a court of justice or elsewhere. That system contemplates him as being the fountain of honor and authority; and from his grace and grant derives all franchises, immunities, and privileges; it is easy to perceive that such a sovereign could not be amenable to a court of justice, or subjected to judicial control and actual constraint. It was of necessity, therefore, that suability became incompatible with such sovereignty. Besides, the prince having all the executive powers, the judgment of the courts would, in fact, be only monitory, not mandatory, to him, and a capacity to be advised is a distinct thing from a capacity to be sued. The same feudal ideas run through all their jurisprudence, and constantly remind us of the distinction between the prince and the subject. No such ideas obtain here; at the Revolution, the sovereignty devolved on the people; and they are truly the sovereigns of the country, but they are sovereigns without subjects(unless the African slaves among us may be so called), and have none to govern but-themselves; the citizens of America are equal as fellow-citizens, and as joint tenants in the sovereignty.

From the differences existing between feudal sovereignties and governments founded on compacts, it necessarily follows that their respective prerogatives must differ. Sovereignty is the right to govern; a nation or state-sovereign is the person or persons in whom that resides. In Europe the sovereignty is generally ascribed to the prince; here it rests with the people; there, the sovereign actually administers the government; here, never in a single instance; our governors are the agents of the people, and at most stand in the same relation to their sovereign, in which the regents in Europe stand to their sovereigns. Their princes have personal powers, dignities, and pre-eminences, our rulers have none but of cial; nor do they partake in the sovereignty otherwise, or in any other capacity, than as private citizens.

Second. The second object of inquiry now presents itself, viz., whether suability is compatible with State sovereignty?

Suability, by whom? Not by a subject, for in this country there are none; not an inferior, for all citizens being as to civil rights perfectly equal, there is not, in that respect, one citizen inferior to another. It is agreed that one free citizen may sue another; the obvious dictates of justice and the purposes of society demanding it. It is agreed, that one free citizen may sue any number on whom process can be conveniently executed; nay, in certain cases one citizen may sue forty thousand; for where a corporation is sued, all the members of it are actually sued, though not personally sued. In this city there are forty odd thousand free citizens, all of whom may be collectively sued by any individual citizen. In the State of Delaware, there are fty odd thousand free citizens, and what reason can be assigned why a free citizen who has demands against them should not prosecute them? Can the difference between forty odd thousand and fifty odd thousand make any distinction as to right? Is it not as easy, and as convenient to the public and parties, to serve a summons on the Governor and Attorney-General of Delaware, as on the Mayor or other of cers of the corporation of Philadelphia? Will it be said, that the fty odd thousand citizens in Delaware being associated under a State government, stand in a rank so superior to the forty odd thousand of Philadelphia associated under their charter, that although it may become the latter to meet an individual on an equal footing in a court of justice, yet that such procedure would not comport with the dignity of the former? In this land of equal liberty, shall forty odd thousand in one place be compellable to do justice, and yet fty odd thousand in another place be privileged to do justice only as they may think proper? Such objections would not correspond with the equal rights we claim; with the equality we profess to admire and maintain, and with that popular sovereignty in which every citizen partakes. Grant that the Governor of Delaware holds an of ce of superior rank to the Mayor of Philadelphia, they are both nevertheless the of cers of the people; and however more exalted one may be than the other, yet in the opinion of those who dislike aristocracy, that circumstance cannot be a good reason for impeding the course of justice.

If there be any such incompatibility as is pretended, whence does it arise? In what does it consist? There is at least one strong, undeniable fact against this incompatibility, and that is this: any one State in the Union may sue another State in this court; that is, all the people of one State may sue all the people of another State. It is plain, then, that a State may be sued, and hence it plainly follows, that suability and State sovereignty are not incompatible. As one State may sue another State in this court, it is plain that no degradation to a State is thought to accompany her appearance in this court. It is not, therefore, to an appearance in this court that the objection points. To what does it point? It points to an appearance at the suit of one or more citizens. But why it should be more incompatible, that all the people of a State should be sued by one citizen, than by one hundred thousand, I cannot perceive, the process in both cases being alike; and the consequences of a judgment alike. Nor can I observe any greater inconveniences in the one case than in the other, except what may arise from the feelings of those who may regard a lesser number in an inferior light. But if any reliance be made on this inferiority as an objection, at least one half its force is done away with by this fact, viz., that it is conceded that a State may appear in this court as plaintiff against a single citizen as defendant; and the truth is, that the State of Georgia is at this moment prosecuting an action in this court against two citizens of South Carolina.

The only remnant of objection, therefore, that remains is that the State is not bound to appear and answer as a defendant at the suit of an individual: but why it is unreasonable that she should be so bound is hard to conjecture. That rule is said to be a bad one which does not work both ways; the citizens of Georgia are content with a right of suing citizens of other States, but are not content that citizens of other States should have a right to sue them.

Let us now proceed to inquire whether Georgia has not, by being a party to the national compact, consented to be suable by individual citizens of another State. This inquiry naturally leads our attention: 1st, To the design of the Constitution. 2d. To the letter and express declaration in it.

Prior to the date of the Constitution, the people had-not any national tribunal to which they could resort for justice; the distribution of justice was then confined to State judicatories, in whose institution and organization the people of the other States had no participation, and over whom they had not the least control. There was then no general court of appellate jurisdiction, by whom the errors of State courts, affecting either the nation at large or the citizens of any other State, could be revised and corrected. Each State was obliged to acquiesce in the measure of justice which another State might yield to her, or to her citizens; and that even in cases where State considerations were not always favorable to the most exact measure. There was danger that from this source animosities would in time result; and as the transition from animosities to hostilities was frequent in the history of independent States, a common tribunal for the termination of controversies became desirable, from motives both of justice and of policy.

Prior also to that period, the United States had, by taking a place among the nations of the earth, become amenable to the laws of nations; and it was their interest as well as their duty to provide that those laws should be respected and obeyed; in their national character and capacity the United States were responsible to foreign nations for the conduct of each State relative to the laws of nations, and the performance of treaties; and there the inexpediency of referring all such questions to State courts, and particularly to the courts of delinquent States, became apparent. While all States were bound to protect each, and the citizens of each, it was highly proper and reasonable that they should be in a capacity not only to cause justice to be done to each, and the citizens of each, but also to cause justice to be done by each and the citizens of each; and that not by violence and force, but in a stable, sedate, and regular course of judicial procedure.

These were among the evils against which it was proper for the nation, that is, the people of all the United States, to provide by a national judiciary, to be instituted
86

by the whole nation, and to be responsible to the whole nation.

Let us now turn to the Constitution. The people therein declare that their design in establishing it comprehended six objects: 1st. To form a more perfect union. 2d. To establish justice. 3d. To insure domestic tranquillity. 4th. To provide for the common defence. 5th. To promote the general welfare. 6th. To secure the blessings of liberty to themselves and their posterity. It would be pleasing and useful to consider and trace the relations which each of these objects bears to the others; and to show that they collectively comprise everything requisite, with the blessing of Divine Providence, to render a people prosperous and happy; on the present occasion such disquisitions would be unseasonable, because foreign to the subject immediately under consideration.

It may be asked, what is the precise sense and attitude in which the words "to establish justice," as here used, are to be understood? The answer to this question will result from the provisions made in the Constitution under this head. They are speci ed in the 2d section of the 3d article, where it is ordained that the judicial power of the United States shall extend to ten descriptions of case—viz.: 1st. To all cases arising under this Constitution; because the meaning, construction, and operation of a compact ought always to be ascertained by all the parties; or by authority derived only from one of them. 2d. To all cases arising under the laws of the United States; because as such laws, constitutionally made, are obligatory on each State, the measure of obligation and obedience ought not to be decided and xed by the party from whom they are due, but by a tribunal deriving authority from both the parties. 3d. To all cases arising under treaties made by their authority; because, as treaties are compacts made by, and obligatory on, the whole nation, their operation ought not to be affected or regulated bythe local laws or courts of a part of the nation. 4th. To all cases affecting ambassadors, or other public ministers and consuls; because, as these are officers of foreign nations, whom this nation is bound to protect and treat according to the laws of nations, cases affecting them ought only to be cognizable by national authority. 5th. To all cases of admiralty and maritime jurisdiction; because, as the seas are the joint property of nations, whose rights and privileges relative thereto are regulated by the law of nations and treaties, such cases necessarily belong to national jurisdiction. 6th. To controversies to which the United States shall be a party; because, in cases in which the whole people are interested, it would not be equal or wise to let any one State decide and measure out justice due to others. 7th. To controversies between two or more States; because domestic tranquillity requires that the contention of States should be peaceably terminated by a common judicatory; and because in a free country justice ought not to depend on the will of either of the litigants. 8th. To controversies between a State and citizens of another State; because, in case a State (that is, all the citizens of it) has demands against some citizens of another State, it is better that she should prosecute their demands in a national court, than in the court of the State to which those citizens belong; the danger of irritation and criminations arising from apprehensions and suspicions of partiality being thereby obviated. Because, in cases where some citizens of one State have demands against all the citizens of another State, the cause of liberty and the rights of men forbid that the latter should be the sole judges of the justice due to the latter; and true republican government requires that free and equal citizens should have free, fair, and equal justice. 9th. To controversies between citizens of the same State claiming lands under grants of different States; because, as the rights of the two States to grant the land are drawn into question, neither of the two States ought to decide the controversy. 10th. To controversies between a State or the citizens thereof; and foreign states, citizens, or subjects; because, as every nation is responsible for the conduct of its citizens towards other nations, all questions touching the justice due to foreign nations or people ought to be ascertained by, and depend on, national authority. Even this cursory view of the judicial powers of the United States leaves the mind strongly impressed with the importance of them to the preservation of the tranquillity, the equal sovereignty, and the equal rights of the people.

The question now before us renders it necessary to pay particular attention to that part of the 2d section which extends the judicial power "to controversies between a State and citizens of another State." It is contended that this ought to be construed to reach none of these controversies, excepting those in which a State may be plaintiff. The ordinary rules for construction will easily decide whether those words are to be understood in that limited sense.

This extension of power is remedial, because it is to settle controversies. It is therefore to be construed liberally. It is politic, wise, and good that not only the controversies in which a State is plaintiff, but also those in which a State is defendant, should be settled; both cases, therefore, are within the reason of the remedy, and ought to be so adjudged, unless the obvious, plain, and literal sense of the words forbid it. If we attend to the words, we nd them to be express, positive, free from ambiguity, and without room for such implied expressions: "The judicial power of the United States shall extend to controversies between a State and citizens of another State." If the Constitution really meant to extend these powers only to those controversies in which a State might be plaintiff, to the exclusion of those in which citizens had demands against a State, it is inconceivable that it should have attempted to convey that meaning in words, not only so incompetent, but also repugnant to it; if it meant to exclude a certain class of these controversies, why were they not expressly excepted; on the contrary, not even an intimation of such intention appears in any part of the Constitution. It cannot be pretended that where citizens urge and insist upon demands against a State, which the State refuses to admit and comply with, that there is no controversy between them. If it is a controversy between them, then it clearly falls not only within the spirit, but the very words of the Constitution. What is it to the cause of justice, and how can it affect the de nition of the word controversy, whether the demands which cause the dispute are made by a State against the citizens of another State, or by the latter against the former? When power is thus extended to a controversy, it necessarily, as to all judicial purposes, is also extended to those between whom it subsists.

The exception contended for would contradict and do violence to the great and leading principles of a free and equal national government, one of the objects of which is to ensure justice to all: to the few against the many as well as to the many against the few. It would be strange, indeed, that the joint and equal sovereigns of this country should, in the very Constitution by which they professed to establish justice, so far deviate from the plain path of equality and impartiality as to give to the collective citizens of one State a right of suing individual citizens of another State, and yet deny to those citizens a right of suing them. We nd the same general and comprehensive manner of expressing the same ideas in a subsequent clause, in which the Constitution ordains that "in all cases affecting ambassadors, other public ministers and consuls, and those in which a state shall be a party, the Supreme Court shall have original jurisdiction." Did it mean here party-plaintiff? If that only was meant, it would have been easy to have found words to express it. Words are to be understood in their ordinary and common acceptation, and the word "party" being incommon usage applicable to plaintiff and defendant, we cannot limit it to one of them in the present case. We find the Legislature of the United States expressing themselves in the like general and comprehensive manner; they speak in the 13th section of the Judicial Act of controversies where a State is a party, and as they do not impliedly or expressly apply that term to either of the litigants in particular, we are to understand them as speaking of both. In the same section they distinguish the cases where Ambassadors are plaintiffs from those in which Ambassadors are defendants, and make different provisions respecting those cases; and it is not unnatural to suppose that they would in like manner have distinguished between cases where a State was plaintiff and where a State was defendant, if they had intended to make any difference between them, or if they had apprehended that the Constitution had made any difference between them.

I perceive, and therefore candor urges me to mention, a circumstance which seems to favor the opposite side of the question. It is this: the same section of the Constitution which extends the judicial power to controversies "between a State and the citizens of another State" does also extend that power to controversies to which the United States are a party. Now it may be said if the word party comprehends both plaintiff and defendant, it follows that the United States may be sued by any citizen between whom and them there may be a controversy. This appears to me to be fair reasoning; but the same principles of candor which urge me to mention this objection also urge me to suggest an important difference between the two cases. It is this: in all cases of actions against States or individual citizens, the national courts are supported in all their legal and constitutional proceedings and judgments by the arm of the executive power of the United States; but in cases of actions against the United States, there is no power which the courts can call to their aid. From this distinction important conclusions are deducible, and they place the case of a State and the case of the United States in very different points of view.

I wish the state of society was so far improved, and the science of government advanced to such a degree of perfection, as that the whole nation could in the peaceable course of law be compelled to do justice and be sued by individual citizens. Whether that is or is not now the case ought not to be thus collaterally and incidentally decided: I leave it a question.

As this opinion, though deliberately formed, has been hastily reduced to writing between the intervals of the daily adjournments, and while my mind was occupied and wearied with the business of the day, I fear it is less concise and connected than it might otherwise have been. I have made no references to cases, because I know of none that are not distinguishable from this case; nor does it appear to me to be necessary to show that the sentiments of the best writers on government and the rights of men harmonize with the principles which direct my judgment on the present question. The acts of the former Congresses, and the acts of many of the State conventions are replete with similar ideas; and to the honor of the United States, it may be observed that, in no other country are subjects of this kind better, if so well, understood. The attention and attachment of the Constitution to the equal rights of the people are discernible in almost every sentence of it; and it is to be regretted that the provision in it which we have been considering, has not in every instance received the approbation and acquiescence which it merits. Georgia has in strong language advocated the cause of republican equality; and there is reason to hope that the people of that State will yet perceive that it would not have been consistent with that equality, to have exempted the body of her citizens from that suability which they are at this moment exercising against citizens of another State.

For my own part, I am convinced that the sense in

which I understand and have explained the words "controversies between States and citizens of another State," is the true sense. The extension of the judiciary power of the United States to such controversies, appears to me to be wise, because it is honest and because it is useful. It is honest because it provides in doing justice without respect of persons, and by securing individual citizens as well as States in their respective rights, performs the promise which every free government makes to every free citizen, of equal justice and protection. It is useful because it is honest, because it leaves not even the most obscure and friendless citizen without means of obtaining justice from a neighboring State; because it obviates occasions of quarrels between States on account of the claims of their respective citizens; because it recognizes and strongly rests on this great moral truth, that justice is the same whether due from one man to a million, or from a million to one man; because it teaches and greatly appreciates the value of our free, republican, national government, which places all our citizens on an equal footing, and enables each and every of them to obtain justice without any danger of being overborne by the weight and number of their opponents; and, because it brings into action and enforces this great and glorious principle, that the people are the sovereign of this country, and consequently that fellow-citizens and joint sovereigns cannot be degraded by appearing with each other in their own courts to have their controversies determined. The people have reason to prize and rejoice in such valuable privileges; and they ought not to forget that nothing but the free course of constitutional law and government can insure the continuance and enjoyment of them.

For the reasons before given, I am clearly of opinion that a State is suable by citizens of another State, but lest I should be understood in a latitude beyond my meaning,

I think it necessary to subjoin this caution, viz.: That

such suability may nevertheless not extend to all the demands and to every kind of action; there may be exceptions. For instance, I am far from being prepared to say that an individual may sue a State on bills of credit issued before the Constitution was established, and which were issued and received on the faith of the State, and at a time when no ideas or expectations of judicial interposition were entertained or contemplated.

DRAFT OF PROCLAMATION OF NEUTRALITY,
BY JOHN JAY
April 11th, 1793.

Whereas every nation has a right to change and modify their constitution and government in such a manner as they may think most conducive to their welfare and happiness, and whereas a new form of government has taken place and actually exists in France, that event is to be regarded as the act of the nation until that presumption shall be destroyed by fact; and although certain circumstances have attended that revolution, which are greatly to be regretted, yet the United States as a nation have no right to decide on measures which regard only the internal and domestic affairs of others. They who actually administer the government of any nation are by foreign nations to be regarded as its lawful rulers so long as they continue to be recognized and obeyed by the great body of their people.

And whereas royalty has been in fact abolished in France, and a new government does there at present exist and is in actual operation, it is proper that the intercourse between this nation and that should be conducted through the medium of the government in fact, and although the misfortunes, to whatever cause they may be imputed, which the late King of France and others have suffered in the course of that revolution, or which that nation may yet experience, are to be regretted by the friends of humanity, and particularly by the people of America to whom both that king and that nation have done essential services, yet it is no less the duty than the interest of the United States strictly to observe that conduct towards all nations which the laws of nations prescribe.

And whereas war actually exists between France on the one side and Austria, Prussia, Great Britain, and the

United Netherlands on the other; and whereas on the one hand we have abundant reason to give thanks unto Almighty God that the United States are not involved in that calamity, so on the other hand it is our duty by a conduct strictly neutral and inoffensive to cultivate and preserve peace, with a rm determination, nevertheless, always to prefer war to injustice and disgrace.

I do therefore most earnestly advise and require the citizens of the United States to be circumspect in their conduct towards all nations and particularly those now at war, to demean themselves in every respect in the manner becoming a nation at peace with all the world, and to unite in rendering thanks to a bene cial Providence for the peace and prosperity we enjoy, and devoutly to entreat the continuance of these-invaluable blessings. I do expressly require that the citizens of the United States abstain from acting hostilely against any of the belligerent powers under commissions from either. Such conduct would tend to provoke hostilities against their country, and would in every respect be highly reprehensible; for while the people of all other states abstain from doing injury to any of our people, it would be unjust and wicked in any of our people to do injuries to them.

I do also enjoin all magistrates and others in authority to be watchful and diligent in preventing any aggressions from being committed against foreign nations and their people; and to cause all offenders to be prosecuted and punished in an exemplary manner. I do also recommend it to my fellow-citizens in general to omit such public discussions as may tend not only to cause divisions and parties among ourselves, and thereby impair that union on which our strength depends, but also give unnecessary cause of offence and irritation to foreign powers. And I cannot forbear expressing a wish that our printers may study to be impartial in the representation of facts, and observe much prudence relative to such strictures and animadversions as may render the disposition of foreign governments and rulers unfriendly to the people of the United States.

CHARGE TO GRAND JURY,
RICHMOND, VIRGINIA

It is an observation no less useful than true, that nations and individuals injure their essential interests in proportion as they deviate from order. By order I mean that national regularity which results from attention and obedience to those rules and principles of conduct which reason indicates and which morality and wisdom prescribe. Those rules and principles reach every station and condition in which individuals can be placed, and extend to every possible situation in which nations can nd themselves.

Among these rules are comprehended the laws of the land, and that they may be so observed as to produce the regularity and order intended by them, courts of justice were instituted whose business it is to punish offences and to render right to those who suffer wrong.

To inquire into and present those offences is the duty which the law generally imposes upon you, and, as there is a national tribunal having cognizance only of offences against the laws of the United States, your inquiries and presentments are to be confined to offences of that description.

The Constitution, the statutes of Congress, the laws of nations, and treaties constitutionally made compose the laws of the United States.

You will perceive that the object is twofold: To regulate the conduct of the citizens relative to our own nation and people, and relative to foreign nations and their subjects.

To the first class belong those statutes which respect trades, navigation, and nance, and those against forgery and counterfeiting and the other offences enumerated in what is generally called the penal statute; to particularize and explain each of those would require details which on this occasion would be unnecessary. Among the most important are those which respect the revenue. Their object is to provide for the payment of debts already accrued, and to provide for the current and for the contingent expenses of the government and nation.

Justice and policy unite in declaring that debts fairly contracted should be honestly paid. On this basis only can public credit be erected and supported; and they either want wisdom or virtue, or both, who regard fraud and chicane as a justi able or useful instrument of policy. The man or the nation who eludes the payment of debts ceases to be worthy of further credit, and generally meets with deserts in the entire loss of it, and in the evils resulting from that loss. The current or ordinary expenses of our government are less than those of any other nation. What our extraordinary expenses may be cannot be foreseen and consequently cannot be calculated. They will depend on events. A war would demand supplies which taxes alone cannot produce and for which recourse must be had to loans. The success of loans will always depend on our credit; and our credit will always be in proportion to our resources, to our integrity, and to our punctuality. All our citizens, therefore, are deeply interested in public credit. It is their duty to unite in preserving and supporting it; and it is your duty, gentlemen, to inquire into and present such violations of the revenue laws as you may nd to have been committed within this district. It gives me pleasure to observe that the respect hitherto paid to those laws by our fellow-citizens in general has been exemplary and honorable to their virtue and patriotism. I hope the result of your inquiries will give additional force to this remark.

The present state of affairs requires that the second object of the laws should be attentively regarded. I mean those which regulate our conduct relative to foreign nations.

This head comprises the laws of nations and treaties.

By the laws of nations our conduct relative to other nations is to be regulated both in peace and in war. It is a subject that merits attention and inquiry, and it is much to be wished that it may be more generally studied and understood.

It may be asked who made the laws of nations? The answer is he from whose will proceed all moral obligations, and which will is made known to us by reason or by revelation.

Nations are, in respect to each other, in the same situation as independent individuals in a state of nature.

Suppose twenty families should be cast on an island and after dividing it between them conclude to remain unconnected with each other by any kind of government, would it thence follow that there are no laws to direct their conduct towards one another? Certainly not. Would not the laws of reason and morality direct them to behave to each other with respect, with justice, with benevolence, with good faith—would not those laws direct them to abstain from violence, to abstain from interfering in their respective domestic government and arrangements, to abstain from causing quarrels and dissensions in each other's families? If they made treaties, would they not be bound to observe them? Or if by consent expressed or implied they gave occasion to usages mutually convenient, would not those usages grow into conventional laws? The answer is obvious.

In like manner the nations throughout the world are like so many great families placed by Providence on the earth, who having divided it between them, remain perfectly distinct from and independent of each other. Between them there is no judge but the great Judge of all. They have a perfect right to establish such governments and build such houses as they prefer, and their neighbors have no right to pull down either because not fashioned according to their ideas of perfection; in a word, one has no right to interfere in the affairs of another, but all are bound to behave to each other with respect, with justice, with benevolence, and with good faith.

When two or more of them are at war about objects in which other nations are not interested, the latter are not to interfere except as mediators and friends to peace; but, on the contrary, ought to observe a strict impartiality towards both, abstaining from affording military aid of any kind or giving just cause of offence to either.

The United States are now in this situation relative to the belligerent powers. Strict impartiality is our duty in all cases where prior treaties do not stipulate for favors, and it is no less our interest than our duty to act accordingly. A just war is an evil, but it is not the greatest; oppression and disgrace are greater. War is not to be sought, but it is not to be ed from. Let us do exactly what is just and right, and then remain without fear, but not without care about the consequences. An unjust war is among the greatest of evils; and for this and numerous other reasons—because the blood and misery caused by it must rest on the heads of those who wage it.

I have mentioned respect among the duties which nations owe to each other. This merits attention. Every man owes it to himself to behave to others with civility and good manners; and every nation in like manner is obliged by a due regard to its own dignity and character to behave towards other nations with decorum. Insolence and rudeness will not only degradeand disgrace nations and individuals but also expose them to hostility and insult. It is the duty of both to cultivate peace and good-will and to this nothing is more conducive than justice, benevolence, and good manners. Indiscretions of this kind have given occasion to many wars.

If in this district you should nd any persons engaged in tting out privateers or enlisting men to serve against either of the belligerent powers, and in other respects violating the laws of neutrality, you will present them. Doubtful cases may arise; on such occasions the attorney-general or the court will afford you the necessary assurance.

But the belligerent powers owe duties to us as well as we to them. They may violate our neutrality and commit offences. If you nd any foreigners in this district committing seditious practices, endeavoring to seduce our citizens into acts of hostility, or attempting to withdraw them from the allegiance of the United States, present them. Such men are guilty of high misdemeanor.

A novel doctrine has been propagated and found some advocates even in this enlightened country—viz., that as citizens have a right to expatriate, so they have a right to engage and enlist in the military service of one of the powers at war, provided they at the same time declare that they expatriate. I make no remarks on this ridiculous doctrine—its absurdity is obvious.

Of national violations of our neutrality our government only can take cognizance. Questions of peace and war and reprisals and the like do not belong to courts of justice, nor to individual citizens, nor to associations of any kind, and for this plain reason: because the people of the United States have been pleased to commit them to Congress.

Are we then to punish our citizens for hostile conduct towards such of the belligerent powers as violate our neutrality and do us injustice? This is a natural question.

There must be order in society or the bonds of it will soon be dissolved. This order consists in every man moving in his own sphere, doing the duties incumbent upon him, and not going out of the circle of his own rights and powers to meddle with or of ciously supervise those of others.

The great question before mentioned being committed exclusively to Congress, they must be left to deliberate, and their decisions must be conclusive.

We have peace with France, Holland, Great Britain, and others, and in case of certain infractions and aggressions on their part the United States, or the department of the government to which they have delegated that authority, have a right to demand satisfaction, and in case of refusal, to declare war or to direct reprisals, or such other measures as circumstances may dictate. But it does not follow from the existence of such infractions that any other body or person in the United States have authority to do the like.

Such measures involve a variety of political considerations, such, for instance, as these: Is it advisable immediately to declare war? Would it be more prudent first to remonstrate, or demand reparation, or direct reprisals? Are we ready for war? Would it be wise to risk it at this juncture, or postpone running that risk until we can be better prepared for it? These and a variety of similar considerations ought to precede and govern the decision of those who annul violated treaties, order reprisals, or declare war.

The nation must either move together or lose its force. Until war is constitutionally declared, the nation and all its members must observe and preserve peace, and do the duties incident to a state of peace. Such at present is our situation, and in that light, gentlemen, you will regard it. As free citizens we have a right to think and speak our sentiments on this subject, in terms becoming freemen—that is, in terms explicit, plain, and decorous. As judges and grand jurors, the merits of those political questions are without our province. Let us faithfully do the duties assigned to our stations. It is yours to inquire into and present all offences against the laws of the United States committed in the district or on the high seas by persons in it. We have the fullest confidence that you will discharge those duties with diligence and impartiality, and without fear, favor, affection, or respect to persons.

CHIEF-JUSTICE JAY AND
ASSOCIATE JUSTICES
TO PRESIDENT WASHINGTON
Philadelphia, 8th August, 1793.

Sir:

We have considered the previous question stated in a letter written by your direction to us by the Secretary of State on the 18th of last month, per the lines of separation drawn by the Constitution between the three departments of the government. These being in certain respects checks upon each other, and our being judges of a court in the last resort, are considerations which afford strong arguments against the propriety of our extra-judicially deciding the questions alluded to, especially as the power given by the Constitution to the President, of calling on the heads of departments for opinions, seems to have been purposely as well as expressly united to the executive departments.

We exceedingly regret every event that may cause embarrassment to your administration, but we derive consolation from the re ection that your judgment will discern what is right, and that your usual prudence, decision, and rmness will surmount every obstacle to the preservation of the rights, peace, and dignity of the United States.

We have the honor to be, with perfect respect, sir, your most obedient and most humble servants.